"Once more, Bavinck speaks today through Parker's well-presented translations focused on the essence of Christianity. Bavinck's study of Christianity is suited to the contemporary landscape as much as it was in the early twentieth century. As Bavinck shows, the most important question is the same as that of every generation: 'What do you make of Christ?' Bavinck compellingly demonstrates that the confession of the apostolic tradition, of the Christ of history as the Christ of faith, and of the resurrection as the destiny of humankind, remains at the center of theology and ministry even in an increasingly apathetic age. For these reasons, this volume is an excellent addition to the Anglophone Bavinck corpus and will be widely enjoyed by both the theologically interested Christian and the curious skeptic."

—Cory Brock, Assistant Minister
St. Columba's Free Church, Edinburgh

" 'Who do you say that I am?' This is the question that Jesus asks his disciples and that pervades the New Testament. It is also the question Herman Bavinck endeavors to answer in this short work. In *What is Christianity*? Bavinck walks through a concise, accessible, and erudite answer to this ever-pressing question. Bavinck demonstrates his vast knowledge in a method that is approachable for anyone. This work will prove to be a valuable resource for anyone who aims to answer the question Jesus posed not only to his disciples but to every person. Parker is to be commended for his work in giving us this gift. His translation is as profound yet as readable as the original."

—Cameron Clausing, Lecturer
Applied Theology and Missional Engagement
Christ College, Sydney

"Another work by Herman Bavinck is available in English, and the timing could not be better. We face what Bavinck faced—how to speak intelligently and compellingly to Christianity's 'cultured despisers.' Bavinck argued that the 'basic ideas of Christianity' correspond to and address the 'ineradicable needs of the human heart.' We need to read this work carefully and ask how we can speak to our world in a way just as clarifying and convincing."

—Tim Keller, Chair

Redee

T0015563

"To those grappling with secularization and contemporary questions concerning Christianity and the church, this short work is remarkably relevant. In a time when contemporary engagement tends toward polarization or indifference, Bavinck brilliantly demonstrates what it means to be rooted, irenic, and faithful. Bavinck invites us to find our ground in faith in Christ as we engage in the complex realities of contemporary ecclesial and social life. Through it all, the book reminds us of the beautiful reality of what it means to find one's life in Christ. This translation brings another wonderful gift from Bavinck to the English-speaking world."

—**Gayle Doornbos**
Assistant Professor of Theology
Dordt University, Sioux Center, Iowa

"If you are looking to engage and critique culture faithfully and thoughtfully with both your head and hands, then this newly translated work by Herman Bavinck is a must-read. From the premise that modernity, and subsequently postmodernity, has 'outgrown Christianity,' Bavinck reminds us that the Triune God of Christianity so masterfully described in his *Reformed Dogmatics* remains the only one who can provide rest for our restless souls. Greg Parker's translation of this simple, yet convicting, work is timely and needed as an apologetic for those outside the church and a balm for those within. *Tolle Lege!*"

—**Dan Hoffstetter, Pastor**
Redeemer Bible Fellowship Church
Topton, Pennsylvania

"Many of us are convinced that while Herman Bavinck wrote from a nineteenth-century context, he speaks with marvelous clarity to our twenty-first century. This fine book confirms that conviction, and we are indebted to Gregory Parker Jr. for making it accessible to us in the English-speaking world. In a time when we are regularly presented with a free-floating Jesus—disconnected from the apostolic witness to his teachings and deeds—Bavinck compellingly points us to a very historical Jesus who was also the heaven-sent Savior and Lord!"

—**Richard J. Mouw, President Emeritus**
Fuller Theological Seminary

"Bavinck is the timely voice needed in our current cultural context of polarization, fear, and outrage. Greg Parker brings to life this accessible and theologically rich work, translated for the first time into English. The resource and wisdom it provides for pastors, teachers, growing Christians, and uncertain seekers is invaluable. Speaking to both intellect and heart, Bavinck winsomely summarizes the whole of Christianity, instructively utilizing the Scriptures and history to force the reader to grapple with 'What do *you* make of Christ?' "

—Douglas Tharp, Senior Pastor
Cornerstone Presbyterian Church
Center Valley, Pennsylvania

"Bavinck's brief work introducing Christianity shows that Reformed theology and ecumenicism can go together. Here, Bavinck surveys the Christian faith from its origins in the biblical witness, through its developments and debates between East and West, Roman Catholicism and the Reformation, to its place within the modern world. Accessible and illuminating, the book provides an antidote to nonhistorical and one-sided descriptions of Christian faith, offering a winsome vindication of Reformation theology even as it locates it within the broader unity of the Christian church. We owe Greg Parker much for his labors to bring this delightful introduction to an Anglophone readership!"

—**Nathaniel Gray Sutanto**
Assistant Professor of Systematic Theology
Reformed Theological Seminary

"Much scholarly attention has been drawn to Herman Bavinck's *Reformed Dogmatics*, *Reformed Ethics*, and other well-known addresses. In fact, his writings consist of many pamphlets and short papers that have not been spotlighted yet carry much of his thought. This book is one of such underexplored writings. Gregory Parker's lucid translation and meticulous editorial work make this book highly valuable. In this little book, we are invited by Bavinck to meditate on Jesus Christ as the center of Christianity and on the Triune God as the heart of the Christian faith."

—**Ximian Xu**
Postdoctoral Research Fellow
Theology and Ethics of A.I.
University of Edinburgh

WHAT IS CHRISTIANITY?

HERMAN BAVINCK

WHAT IS CHRISTIANITY?

TRANSLATED & EDITED BY
GREGORY PARKER JR.

HENDRICKSON ACADEMIC

an imprint of Hendrickson Publishing Group

What Is Christianity?

© 2022 Gregory Parker Jr.

Published by Hendrickson Publishers
an imprint of Hendrickson Publishing Group
Hendrickson Publishers, LLC
P. O. Box 3473
Peabody, Massachusetts 01961-3473
www.hendricksonpublishinggroup.com

ISBN 978-1-68307-420-5

Printed in the United States of America

First Printing — March 2022

Cover canvas background texture by slobo / iStock / Getty Images Plus via Getty Images. Cover flower by ulimi / DigitalVision Vectors via Getty Images.

Cover design by Karol Bailey.

Library of Congress Control Number: 2021952235

To Mark Evans, my *pater ecclesia*

and

James Eglinton, my *doktorvater*

Contents

Translator's Preface

Herman Bavinck (1854–1921) was a Dutch Reformed theologian, ethicist, statesman, and Christian. His published writing spans several fields: theology, pedagogy, ethics, psychology, biography, sociology, and so on. By the turn of the twentieth century, he was one of the best-known theologians in the Netherlands, particularly on account of his four-volume *Reformed Dogmatics*.[1] His work continues to be published and read today in multiple languages.

This volume contains two works by Bavinck. The first, "Christianity" (*Het Christendom*), was originally published in 1912 in a series titled Great Religions (*Groote Godsdiensten*).[2] This series had the explicit purpose of providing the Dutch public with an introduction to the primary features of the various religions of the early twentieth century. This book can be viewed as one of Bavinck's contributions to discussions oriented around "the essence of Christianity,"[3] which was a popular theological discussion at that time. "Christianity" is also a prime example of Bavinck's widening theological horizon, alongside other writings such as *Guidebook for Instruction in the Christian Religion*.[4] In both works, Bavinck remained a consummate Reformed theologian, yet his approach to engaging religious and theological conversation in the public sphere took on a more ecumenical focus.[5]

Following "Christianity" is Bavinck's 1883 essay "The Christian Faith" (*Het Christelijk Geloof*).[6] This shorter piece is reflective of Bavinck's early developments of a theological system and contains many features that are characteristic of Bavinck's more mature work: that is, clear cultural observation, concise theological insights, and a system attuned to development. Moreover, it is explicitly creedal. Many of the salient themes of both "Christianity" and "The Christian Faith" can be traced to his magnum opus *Reformed Dogmatics* and then to *Guidebook for Instruction in the Christian Religion.* It is Christ-centered and yet articulates a triune-arc to the Christian life: all things are from, through, and to the Triune God. In "Christianity," he writes of Christ as Christianity itself, and in "The Christian Faith," he describes Christ as the center of all its knowledge and faith.

Readers may see a natural progression to move from reading about the *phenomena* of Christianity to considering more closely its *essence.* In "The Christian Faith," he fleshes out the basic contours of the content, character, and foundation of Christian belief. The reader is introduced to Christianity as a religion that orbits Christ within a cosmic triune system.

We might juxtapose this compilation of Bavinck's work, *What Is Christianity?*, with Rowan Williams's book of the same title.[7] The archbishop of Canterbury from 2002 to 2012, Williams is a highly esteemed Anglican theologian. Both Williams and Bavinck are internationally recognized theologians who have garnered attention for their irenic, erudite, and doxological/theological spirits.

In his book, Williams approaches Christianity through three angles: the *practices* of Christianity, the *faith* of Christianity, and the *fruit* of Christianity. Alternatively, Bavinck's "Christianity" is split into six sections: the *question* of Christianity, the *Jesus* of Christianity, the *confession* of Christianity, the *diversity* of Christianity, the *rise of modernity* and Christianity, and the *respite* of Christianity. Bavinck's method is historical. He guides the reader through church history from the Gospels to the turn of the twentieth century considering the nature of Christianity.

The first section leads the reader into the main theological and religious question of the day, "Who is Jesus?"[8] This includes an introduction to the Quest for the Historical Jesus, which sets the reader up for the implicit argument of the book: Those who reject the *phenomena* of Christianity ultimately turn away from its *essence*, and the denial of Christianity, even in its various forms, is an ultimate rejection of the one person who binds it together—Jesus Christ.[9] As Bavinck writes in his *Reformed Dogmatics:*

> Those who truly accept the apostolic witness trust in Christ alone for their salvation; and those who put their trust in Christ as the Son of God also freely and readily accept the apostolic witness concerning that Christ. The two together, subjectively speaking, constitute the essence of Christianity.[10]

Bavinck's argument concludes that the historical Jesus is the Jesus of the Gospels. In other words, these apostles recorded in the Scriptures a dependable account of who Jesus is. The great early church theologian Augustine makes a similar argument in Book XXII of *The City of God.* He writes about the incredible nature of the pagan world being persuaded by the lowly Christians of the world, who believe in the amazing resurrection and ascension of Jesus Christ. On account of the educated of the world being persuaded by the unlearned, Augustine argues that it necessitates a harder look at the miracle these men enact. In other words, the phenomena of rapid church expansion requires that we reevaluate the person of Jesus. In the more philosophical language of phenomena and essence, Bavinck lifts this argument from the pages of Christian history.[11]

In the second section, Bavinck recapitulates the life of Jesus, beginning with John the Baptist's heralding of the coming Messiah. Bavinck attempts to bring together the overall unity of Scripture with the unfolding of one story from the Old Testament to the New Testament. The diversity of the various Gospel accounts does not conflict with the trustworthiness of Scripture and is rather a compilation of distinct testimonies of faith. One can also see a glimmer of Bavinck's ecumenical focus echoing Ephesians 4:4–6.[12] Concerning the congregations that were originally ministered to by the apostles, he writes:

> They all had one Lord, one faith, one baptism; one God and Father of all, above all and in all; and one Spirit, by whom they were all built together on the foundation of the apostles and prophets into a dwelling place of God.[13]

Truly, this ecumenical emphasis is also present in Bavinck's *Reformed Dogmatics*. There, he does not consider the unity of the church to be rooted in the "institution" of the church but rather the unity of the "organism."[14] Indeed, "unity" is the first of five attributes of the church, which is founded upon the headship of Christ (Eph. 1:10; 5:23). Through the one Spirit, (1 Cor. 6:17–19; 12:13; 2 Cor. 12:18; Eph. 4:4), believers have fellowship with Christ and with one another. This unity is primarily spiritual in character, composed of the unity of faith, hope, love, and baptism (Eph. 4:3–5). According to Bavinck, that which unites Christians is far greater than that which separates them.[15]

In the third section, Bavinck begins to unfold the growth of the Christian confessions by walking through the history of Christianity with the development of the Nicene Creed, which was further fortified at Chalcedon against attacks. He walks the reader through the development of Christian doctrine from the early church through the Reformation.

Along with his focus on doctrine, he intertwines in his narrative a description of the nature of the Christian life. We should not side-step Bavinck's dual emphasis of head and heart. For we see here not only the activity of a theologian carefully articulating the doctrinal side of religion, but also one who advances theology's true role of promoting the living of Christianity itself. Here, he is critical of developments both in the Eastern Church (Greek Orthodox) and the Western Church (Roman Catholicism), where he believes doctrine has negatively impacted life.

In the fourth section, his narrative of the history of Christianity continues with the development of Protestantism as he distinguishes its forefathers—Ulrich Zwingli, John Calvin, and Martin Luther—from one another. In demarcating these three major players, he pays close attention to both doctrine and life, head and heart, and theology and ethics. In this respect, Bavinck believes that Calvin worked out the principles of the Reformation with the greatest purity: "In principle, asceticism belongs on Roman soil, Pietism can appeal to Luther, but Puritanism is a brainchild of Calvin."[16] This simple acknowledgement testifies to Bavinck's continued trajectory as a Reformed theologian, while being an advocate for Christianity writ large.[17]

In the fifth section, Bavinck continues plotting the history of Christianity, which brings him to the eighteenth century. The Reformation brought with it the growth of various other ecclesial movements, including the resurgence of Catholicism.[18] A new set of cultural issues for the church then arose through the rise of Deism and Rationalism, followed by the birth of modernity. This final section ultimately allows Bavinck then to address the newest philosophical issues that were facing the church in his day.

In the concluding section, Bavinck briefly considers the complexity of the nineteenth century, capturing the modern spirit in what would later become known as the "secularization thesis." He writes, "In a word, Christianity has had its time; we have outgrown it completely, we are, insofar as we are modern cultural people, no longer Christians."[19] The modern human, however, is restless. Nothing is easy for the Bavinckian soul. Therefore, Bavinck's response to this is threefold: (1) culture alone does not satisfy the human soul, (2) science's bravado has not been matched by its research, and (3) culture continues to benefit only a few. In this respect, art turned toward symbolism and religion, science became more modest in its claims, and religion did not vanish as many suspected it would. He then returns to the central question: *"What does one make of Christ?"*

If we return to our comparison with Rowan Williams, we can shed more light on Bavinck's work. In the first chapter of Williams's book, he entertains the unity of the church via its practices: prayer, the centrality of the Scriptures, the sacraments, and the life of the Christian.[20] Throughout history, these various practices or forms can be found in nearly every Christian church, although they all to some degree include teaching that is distinct for them in these practices—as Bavinck illustrates through various traditions regarding, for example, the sacraments. Whereas Williams observes the phenomena of *religious practice*, Bavinck observes the historical phenomena of the *church*. Both paint a picture of a church where there is the potential for unity.[21]

Bavinck and Williams are also both concerned with the relationship between faith and life, dogma and ethics, and creed and deed. Williams's final section concerns the payoff of Christianity: that is, does it make any difference if someone believes in Jesus in this world? Bavinck, on the other hand, is concerned with the existential wrestling of the heart. While Bavinck and Williams nuance their answers differently, the Christian church is by and large united in its response to the question, "What does one make of Christ?" Bavinck believes that the Triune God is the only one who can provide rest for humanity's restless souls, and this is his ultimate answer.

Readers may also notice that the Augustinian theme of the restlessness of the heart pervades "The Christian Faith." In both "Christianity" and "The Christian Faith," we are directed to find our rest in the Triune God who is both transcendent and immanent, who providentially oversees all things, yet who knows the number of hairs on our heads. In this God, salvation is certain, which ushers into our lives not a peace or rest that is far-off, but a rest, joy, peace, and satisfaction that believers can experience even now.

If you are a Christian, this volume might be a helpful reminder of the confession of faith that you share with all other Christians:

There is "one Lord, one faith, one baptism, one God and father of all" (Eph. 4:3–5). If you are not a Christian, this book will provide you with a condensed retelling of the history of Christianity and the overarching unity of the Christian faith: the essence of Christianity is the person and work of Christ.[22]

But most importantly, it leaves all readers to wrestle with the all-important question: "What do *you* make of Christ?" Alongside Williams, Bavinck ultimately claims that the God of Christianity—the Father, Son, and Holy Spirit—is the only one who can meet the needs of the human heart. It is the confession of this God that is at the heart of the Christian faith.[23]

Concerning the Translation

Bavinck's original work contained no footnotes or endnotes. All of these have been provided by the editor with a twofold purpose: (1) to provide citations to the works of various theologians, historians, philosophers whom Bavinck references; and (2) to furnish the book with Scripture references to those passages for which Bavinck offers no citation.

Other editorial notations to be aware of include the addition of chapter divisions in "Christianity" and the inclusion of the original Dutch pagination in brackets. The occasional word is placed in a bracket as well. Although these words are not original to the text, they should facilitate a smoother reading experience.[24]

ACKNOWLEDGMENTS

The Christian life is one of humble gratitude. I am above all grateful to be known and loved by Christ. We are always dependent upon God, and always sustained and nourished by his Spirit. I am grateful for my various Christian communities during the translation of this book, namely: St. Columba's Free Church in Edinburgh, Scotland; Christ the King in Cambridge, Massachusetts; and Cornerstone Presbyterian Church in Center Valley, Pennsylvania. The friendship, fellowship, and love of these believers have sustained me through a difficult season.

I am also thankful for those who have been intimately involved in making this translation come to life. First and foremost, thank you to Dr. Richard Lints for providing the afterword. I am pleased that our last collaborative project is no longer moving a tree in your yard! I am also grateful for Art and Shirl Werner, who furnished me with the time and space to complete this translation. I would like to also express my sincerest gratitude to those who helped improve the value of the project: to Alec Simpson, Dr. Cameron Clausing, and Dr. Ty Kieser for evaluating various drafts of the preface and to Henry J. Hoekstra for his work on the index. A heartfelt thanks as well to the staff at Hendrickson Publishers. Thank you in particular to Kate Walker and Patricia Anders for their keen editorial eyes. A sincere thanks to Annemarie de Roos and Dr. Marinus de Jong for providing feedback on the translation. I am reminded of Bavinck's correspondences with his international network of friends and am grateful for the Advanced Theological Studies Fellowship (ATSF) of Theological University Kampen, whose promotion of Reformed international knowledge exchange nurtured the opportunity for such a translation. Any blemishes that remain are my own.

Dr. Albert Cheng, Trevor and Susy Smith, Jacolien van Eekeren, Camille Simpson, Dr. Alastair and Sue Simison, Dan Hoffstetter, Tom Shorb, Dr. Bruce Pass, and Greg Parker Sr. each deserve a special mention for their support and encouragement in this project.

Above all, I would like to thank my *pater ecclesia*, Mark Evans, and my *doktorvater*, James Eglinton, for their friendships and the distinct roles they have played in the cultivation of my Christian life.

Gregory Parker Jr.
Barto, Pennsylvania

Review of "Groote Godsdiensten: Serie II, No. 7. Het Christendom door Dr. H. Bavinck"

It is no small task which Dr. Bavinck has undertaken, to tell in sixty-two small pages all that Christianity is, and that, in a series in which it is brought into comparison with other "great religions." He has fulfilled this task, however, in a most admirable manner. His method is, first, to point out what all Christians are agreed upon; and then to give an historical account of Christianity in its origins and in its progressive manifestations in the great forms of the Orthodox Eastern, the Romish, the Lutheran, Reformed Churches, with further descriptions of the forms it has taken since, in Anabaptism and Socinianism, and the New Protestantism rooted in the Enlightenment. His plan thus resolves itself into an informal sketch of the historical development of Christianity. This sketch is written with remarkable grasp of details and an equally remarkable power of synthesis. We cannot imagine how the work could be done better.

B. B. Warfield
The Princeton Theological Review (1913)

CHRISTIANITY
HET CHRISTENDOM
(1912)

1

The *Question* of Christianity

[3] It may well be a precarious undertaking to provide in a mere handful of pages a description of Christianity that is somewhat sufficient. The richness of [Christianity] is already in inverse proportion to the limitations of the available space. Christianity is a religion which, apart from its beginnings in Israel, has existed for more than eighteen centuries and has in this time gone through a very important history, taken root among various peoples and in distant countries, and has now spread to more than a third of mankind. However, anyone who gave a short and therefore unsatisfactory account of this history would have accomplished only a small part of the task that had been assigned to him in describing Christianity.

For Christianity has an objective side in doctrine and church, in worship and church government. But it also penetrates subjectively into the human being himself; into his mind, heart, and conscience; and there it cultivates a new world of ideas, conditions, and dispositions which are difficult to know and to describe. And from within, the Christian faith again extends to all areas of human life, exerts its influence in all spheres, and leaves [4] its mark on all elements of culture. A description of Christianity that would be satisfactory in any way would have to take into account this inner power and do justice to this hidden, spiritual activity.

This difficult task could perhaps be accomplished today if there were some agreement on the matter itself—that is, on the origin and essence of Christianity. But precisely the opposite is true. From the beginning, different ideas about the nature and character of Christianity were formed; within and alongside the official church, all sorts of groups and sects arose which held a different view of Christianity from that which the majority held. This process of differentiation continued throughout the Middle Ages, expanded still further during and after the Reformation, and has had such a disintegrating effect at the present time that not only do hundreds of churches and sects stand side by side, but practically every thinking person has his own opinion about the Christian religion. Everything that seemed certain in the past is now being questioned, and this doubt is spreading ever wider; not a single word, not a single event reported in the New Testament remains untouched. In recent years, people have even denied and disputed the historical existence of the one after whom Christianity was named. It is obvious that a short description of Christianity cannot meet all the above requirements and cannot discuss and judge all the views expressed; it must be content to give a brief and clear account of the origin and development of the Christian religion.

It cannot be objected that in the series *Groote Godsdiensten*, the Christian religion is treated by someone who was born and raised in it himself, and [5] who therefore considers a certain view of this religion to be the right one or at least the most correct one. Whether he describes Christianity from a Roman, Lutheran, Reformed, or any other Christian point of view, Christianity is for him always a religion in which he has a personal interest. He is not indifferent to it and does not look at it objectively, but he is at the center of it and thinks and lives from it. And this is ultimately the case with all who bear the name of Christian; they all consider that the truth of their conception of Christianity more or less concerns the peace of their hearts, the comfort of their consciences, and the rest of their souls. Even those who answer the question "Are we still Christians?" in the negative are by no means above this personal interest, but it works in another direction and drives them to oppose Christianity; the side of deniers also has its fanatics. That is why it is fortunate that impartiality is not the same as indifference; hate blinds but love often makes things clearer to see.

One thing can somewhat console us in the face of all these difficulties: the division in the understanding of Christianity is indeed great, but not so large that any further reasoning would be superfluous and useless. There are indeed innumerable formulations of the essence of Christianity: the Greek, Roman, Lutheran, Reformed, etc., to which one can add those of Kant and Hegel, of Schleiermacher and Ritschl, of Harnack and Eucken, of Green and Caird, and many others.[1] Yet on several points, there still exists agreement which should be gratefully acknowledged.

In the first place, there is no church or movement that wholly identifies its view of Christianity with the original Christianity.[2] It is true [6] that each party holds its own interpretation to be correct and defends it as such against all others, but nevertheless every church and each movement distinguishes between the truth which has appeared in Christ and the understanding which it has gained of it and which it has, imperfectly and fallaciously, expressed in its confession. The Roman Church is an exception to this, in that it attributes infallibility to the pope and presents its doctrine as the only true and absolutely correct interpretation of the gospel. But it also distinguishes between Christ and the pope as his vice-regent, between the inspiration of the apostles and the assistance of the Holy Spirit, which the head of the church enjoys. In principle, no one disputes the difference between the truth of Scripture and the teaching of the church. This remark is not without significance in regard to those who call their own personal interpretation of the gospel the historical one, as distinct from the dogmatic one given by the churches. Churches, too, have sincerely and earnestly desired in their confession to give as pure an understanding of the gospel as possible. Men like Harnack, for example, who reject this understanding and offer their own explanation also never succeed beyond giving an understanding of the original gospel, which in their view is preferable to all others. Therefore, they do not substitute the gospel for ecclesiastical teaching, but place a different conception of the gospel beside that which is held in the churches. The dispute is not over historical or dogmatic interpretation, but over the facts themselves; that is, over what indeed was the original gospel.

Second, there is also great agreement that the question of the essence of Christianity coincides with that of the original, real and true [7] Christianity, and that to know this we must go back to the Scriptures, especially to the New Testament. Besides, no other sources are available. Josephus's testimony about Jesus is critically suspect and contains nothing new; the slanders spread by the Jews since the middle of the second century to combat Christianity have been welcomed by Celsus, Porphyrius, and more recently by [Ernst] Haeckel, but are not considered in any serious study of original Christianity.[3] The short statements on Christ and the Christians by Tacitus, Suetonius, and Pliny are in themselves important and place the historical existence of Jesus beyond reasonable doubt, but they do not increase our knowledge of early Christianity. And the numerous apocryphal Gospels, which originated in Ebionite and gnostic circles, reveal the desire to be able to say something more about Jesus' life other than what is reported in the four canonical Gospels, and to support one's own dissenting opinions with them rather than to be used as real sources. Only a few of the sayings of Jesus discovered in recent times may have flowed from his lips and been preserved purely by tradition. Apart from these few sources, we have no other sources for the knowledge of the life of Jesus than the books of the New Testament, and even more so the four Gospels, because what is mentioned in the other writings of the New Testament about that life is relatively little and almost entirely contained in the Gospels as well.

With regard to the authenticity, integrity, and reliability of these canonical Gospels, a considerable struggle has been going on for more than a century and a half, and it is not to be expected that it will lead to a universally accepted outcome in the near future. But here are three [8] remarkable things.

First, the attempt should be called a failure to explain Christianity—as it is understood in the churches and expressed centrally in their Christology—from Hellenistic or other alien influences in the second century. The New Testament writings, especially the four main letters of Paul, continue to oppose this and cannot have originated in or after that time. As a result, it is now generally recognized that the church's Christology had its origins in the first century. This then eliminates the reason for moving the various New Testament writings to the second century; successively, they have all been brought back to the first century. In 1897, Harnack said that there had been a time when the oldest Christian literature was regarded as a tapestry of hoaxes and forgeries.[4] But that time is over. We are returning to the traditional [view]. The chronological order in which tradition has arranged the documents, from the letters of Paul to the writings of Irenaeus, is correct in all essential aspects. And this judgment of the Berlin professor has since been more and more confirmed and recognized as correct.

Second, it has not been possible to excavate down to the bottom of the New Testament as low and as deep as all the layers of the earth until one arrives at the rocky foundation of reality. The slogan "From Paul to Jesus, back to the Jesus of the Synoptic Gospels" has proven vain, because the image of Christ is essentially the same in all New Testament writings.[5] How would Paul have come by his teaching about Christ? How could he, with this "falsification" of the original gospel, have found acceptance among the congregations? How could he, expounding his gospel to the apostles in Jerusalem, have received from them the right hand of the [9] community (Gal. 2:2, 9) if he had cherished an entirely different idea in this central article of faith? There was a difference between Paul and some of

his Jewish brethren, but this difference was limited to the consequences arising from the gospel in regard to the Old Testament law
[Gal. 2:11–14]. But there was no difference concerning the person
of Christ, his life, death, resurrection, and return. All the apostles
agreed with one another; there was no question of a christological dispute between them or in the earliest churches. Conversely,
the first three Gospels were written by disciples of Jesus just as the
Gospel of John and the Epistles of Paul were written at a time when
there were already many congregations and for an audience that
had already been taught about the person of Christ by the apostles.
They do not proclaim any Jesus as the Christ other than the one
preached by all the apostles and confessed by all the believers of
that time.

If, however, the earliest church, as far back as we can tell from
the sources, professed Jesus as the Christ, then only two explana-
tions remain: (1) Christ is the product of the church, or (2) the
church is the product of Christ. In the first case, we must imagine
that a group of religious people had existed for a long time, or that
as a result of social circumstances such a group had formed in
that time, who combined the various characteristics present in the
image of Christ in the New Testament from various Hellenistic or
Jewish, Indian, Babylonian, or Egyptian sources and applied them
to a Jesus [figure] who may or may not have existed. Although this
attempt at an explanation has found many supporters in recent
times, it does not seem daring to predict it has little prospect. For
[10] although it offers ample scope for fantasy, it has no basis in
reality. It leaves unanswered the questions as to what brought together this group of persons, from where, simple-minded as they
were, they derived the features of the figure of Christ, how they
were able to link them to such a harmonious image as we see in
the New Testament, how they came to think of all of them in a
certain man Jesus, the reason why they believed in the existence
of this Jesus, etc. The riddles are so numerous that no other con-

clusion remains than this: without Christ, Christianity cannot be explained.

And this is also a third point on which there is fairly general agreement. There are many who have broken with Christianity once and for all and who no longer care about the person of Christ. But this indifference is also significant, for it tacitly implies the recognition that the Christ of the church is identical with the Christ of the Scriptures, and that through reduction and criticism no Jesus is to be found in the Gospels who still delights their hearts. Besides, the whole attempt to explain the Christ of the New Testament through pagan influences, which is attempted by many today, is based on the same concession and is an eloquent vindication of the church's creed. Fortunately, however, not all those who reject the Christology of Paul and John are pursuing this indifference. They still value the Christian name and feel connected to the person of Jesus. That is why they strive to give him an exceptional place in the kingdom of God. They accept a special revelation of God in him and believe that in his person and work he has a lasting significance for the religious and ethical development of [11] mankind. Even in this weak form, their confession serves as proof that the question of the origin and essence of Christianity is identical with that of the person and work of Christ. *What do you think of Christ?* This is and remains the primary question in religion and theology.

2

The *Jesus* of Christianity

Toward the end of the fifteenth year of the reign of the emperor Tiberias (779, after the foundation of Rome, and 26 or 27 of the Christian era), when Herod Antipas was king of Galilee and Peraea, and Pontius Pilate was governor of Judea, a remarkable religious revival took place among the Jews. At that time, suddenly, from the deserts of Judah a man emerged with the marks of a harsh lifestyle on his face, wearing nothing but a rough coat of camel hair fastened to his loins by a leather belt, and calling out to all who would hear him that they must repent, for the kingdom of heaven was at hand [Matt. 3:1–12]. With this preaching, John, later called the Baptist, followed in the footsteps of the ancient prophets who had also repeatedly urged their people to repent. But he urged them on with the prophecy that the long-awaited kingdom of heaven was now at hand. It is true that the Old Testament already taught that God is king of the whole earth (Ps. 24; 29; Jer. 10: 7, etc.), and that since the establishment of his covenant on Sinai he has been, in a special sense, king of his people Israel (Isa. 33: 22); but that kingship of God was in the course of history less and less recognized and more and more seriously resisted by the people. If that kingship of God on earth was to be realized at all, it could not happen in the way of gradual development, but it had to come down suddenly from above, by a special act of God's salvation and power. Therefore, it became [12] more and more the prayer and expectation of the people of Israel that God would rend the heavens and through his own descent reveal his righteousness and salvation (Isa. 64:1, etc.). Daniel, in particular, elaborated on this idea: after the world empires, the kingdom of God will descend from above. The four preceding kingdoms are like four animals coming up out of the sea, out of the world of nations from below; but after that there is a kingdom, represented as a stone hewn without hands out of the mountain, and itself becoming a great mountain [Dan. 7:17–18]. It is a kingdom which the God of heaven will bring about and which will not be disturbed (Dan. 2:34–35, 44–45) that will be given to the people of the saints (Dan. 7:18, 27) through the mediation of One, who comes with the clouds of heaven and who is like a son of man (Dan. 7:13). That is why the Jews later named this kingdom the kingdom of heaven, because it would come from above and descend to earth from heaven (cf. John 18:36).

John the Baptist announced the coming of that kingdom, and he added that it would not come through Abrahamic descent, or circumcision, or legal righteousness, but only through repentance, a transformation of the mind, a religious-ethical renewal of the soul that opened the entrance to that kingdom. He confirmed this with the baptism which he was commanded by God to administer to all those who came to him with a confession of guilt, as a sign and seal of their conversion and of the great blessing of forgiveness, which was both the condition and the content of the kingdom of heaven.

With this preaching, John made a powerful impression. The Pharisees and Sadducees took a critical stance against him and were therefore addressed by him in severe language and threatened with judgment (Matt. 3:7–12), but the people flocked to him from all sides—from [13] Jerusalem and all Judea and the whole land around the Jordan, and they were baptized by him, confessing their sins (Matt 3:5–6; 21:32). Many also came to him from Galilee (Matt. 11:7–9), and among them was Jesus, the son of Joseph and Mary, who was born in Bethlehem and brought up in Nazareth (Mark 1:9), and who came specifically to John with the intention of being baptized by him (Matt. 3:13). This baptism had great significance not only for Jesus but also for John. For hitherto he had declared as strongly as possible that he himself was not the Messiah, but that a mightier one would come after him, whose shoes he was not worthy to untie, and who would baptize with the Holy Spirit and with fire (Matt. 3:13). The general testimony, which had hitherto been given by John and is to be found in the Synoptic [Gospels], now takes on a special character and designates Jesus as the Son of God and the Lamb who takes away the sin of the world, as the Fourth Gospel particularly mentions [John 1:29].

But this baptism also marked a turning point in the life of Jesus. Little is known to us of his childhood and early adulthood. We are only told that he was conceived of the Holy Spirit and born of the virgin Mary; that he was circumcised on the eighth day and presented to the Lord a few weeks later in the temple; that later he went with his parents to Jerusalem every year on feast days; and that already as a twelve-year-old boy, he testified that he had to be among the things (or in the house) of his Father [Luke 2]. However, after his baptism, which was the confirmation of his sonship, the anointing with God's Spirit and the qualification for his ministerial activity, he soon ministered in public among his people.

The word that [Jesus] spoke was the same as John: "The time is fulfilled, and the kingdom of God is at hand; [14] repent and believe the gospel" (i.e. the kingdom of God, Mark 1:15). That was the theme of his teaching, but he worked it out more comprehensively and deeply than John or any of the prophets before him possibly could. The kingdom of God is first and foremost a gift that descends from above and is given according to God's will to those for whom it was prepared before the foundation of the world, and thus it can only be received by childlike faith [Matt. 6:33; 4:17; 5:19; 7:21; 16:19; 19:14]. Yet it must also be sought out by people (though not as a moral good) and valued as a treasure or a pearl above all things [Matt. 13:44–45]. To the extent that it can already be received here on earth and that the goods of that kingdom—truth, righteousness, forgiveness of sins, peace, life—can already be enjoyed today, it is already present. As Satan's power is being destroyed, it is realized here on earth. That is why the kingdom is like a seed or a sourdough, which gradually develops [Matt. 13:31]. It will, however, only be fully realized in the future, when the heirs will receive eternal life in heaven, share in the reward for their struggles and efforts, and all will sit together at the feast that is being prepared by the Father.

The only path that leads to that kingdom and within that kingdom to the constant enjoyment of its goods is that of faith and conversion, regeneration and self-denial, bearing one's cross and following Jesus. One must give one's all for that kingdom, houses and fields, parents and children; one must even pluck out one's eye and cut off one's hand and foot if they are an obstacle. It becomes the property only of the pure of heart, the peaceful, the merciful, etc. And these citizens of the kingdom are also children of the Father, who is in heaven, and among themselves brothers; the fulfillment of God's will fashions them into a [15] new family, into a congregation set apart from the world, which has only one Master, and in his name is led and governed by the apostles [Matt. 19:13–30].

The most remarkable thing in the teachings of Jesus, however, is the place he accords himself in the kingdom of heaven. [Jesus] is perfect and truly human, who describes himself as meek and humble, who depends on and is subject to the Father in everything, who continually withdraws into solitude in order to seek strength in prayer. The day and hour of the future of the kingdom of God are unknown to him; the decision making about the positions in that kingdom is not up to him but belongs to the Father [Matt. 2:20–27]; he calls his father's decision making good,[1] and he himself has come to serve and to suffer. At the same time, his whole appearance and conduct, all his words and deeds, are based on such a powerful and exalted self-consciousness that everyone gets the impression that he exceeds all people by a great distance.[2] And that self-consciousness is often expressed in a self-testimony that would be considered pride when it comes to any other person.[3] Already this is remarkable, that he calls himself meek and humble of heart, without anyone daring to get irritated by it.

Although he is a human being in everything, he also knows himself to be more than human at all times. Already as a twelve-year-old, he is conscious of an intimate fellowship with the Father, and he says that he has to be occupied with his things. And that fellowship is never disturbed and never broken. With him there is no question of falling down and getting up, of faltering and standing up; his prayer, even in the deepest and heaviest suffering, never includes a confession of sin or a plea for forgiveness. He is greater than Jonah and Solomon [Matt. 12:38–42], greater than the angels [Heb. 1:4–6], and greater than the temple [Matt.12:6].

Blessed are the eyes that see what his disciples see [Matt. 13:16; Luke 10:23]; the least in the kingdom of heaven is greater than John the Baptist, who was the foremost among [16] those born of women [Matt. 11:11]. [Jesus] is Lord of the Sabbath and establishes it as his: I say unto you, over against all the scribes [Matt. 12:1–8; Mark 2:23–28; Luke 6:1–5]. He distributes all the goods of the kingdom himself and has the power to forgive sins, which, according to the belief of the Jews, belongs to God alone. He walks through the land, healing and alleviating all sickness and disease among the people and raises the dead solely by his word of power. He is the Father's own son, in contrast to all servants, to whom has been given everything that belongs to the establishment of the kingdom of God and to whom only the Father can lead and accept into his fellowship.

He is not just a prophet who testifies about the kingdom of God, but he is the king of it, who brings it about through the works he performs in the Spirit of God, and who makes it available to others as it has been made available to him by the Father. The relationship in which people place themselves to him determines their fate or salvation. Whoever confesses him before men, he will confess before his Father in heaven [Matt. 10:32–33; Luke 12:8]. He who is ashamed of him and does not forsake everything for his sake and for the sake of the gospel cannot be his disciple and is not worthy of him [Mark 8:38; Luke 9:26]. He cries out woe over Capernaum and Bethsaida and Jerusalem, because they have not accepted him [Matt. 11:20–24; Luke 10:12–16]. After he has finished his earthly mission, he takes his place at the right hand of God and will return on the clouds in glory, as the judge of the whole world, to judge all and to repay each according to their works [Matt. 24:29–31; 2 Tim. 4:1].

This powerful self-consciousness implies nothing less than that he stands in a wholly unique relationship with the Father and is, in a special sense, his Son, which forms the foundation of his messiahship. In recent times, it has been argued that Jesus himself did not claim to be the Messiah, but that it was only through faith in his resurrection that the congregation came to [17] ascribe this title to him. But this sentiment is contradicted by the facts. One only has to think of the entrance into Jerusalem [Matt. 21:1–11; Mark 11:1–11; Luke 19:28–44; John 12:12–19], of Jesus' confession before the Sanhedrin and Pilate [Matt. 26:63–65; 27:1–26; Mark 15:1–15; Luke 1:25; John 18:28–40; 19:1–22], of the mocking of the soldiers [Matt. 27:27–34], and of the inscription above his cross [John 19:19–20], all of which cannot be relegated to the realm of fables in any sense. And it was not only later, at the end of his life or only after Caesarea Philippi, that he became aware of this messiahship, but we already find it in him as a twelve-year-old boy in the temple [Luke 2:22–38]; in the baptism administered by John, he received the divine sign and seal of [his messiahship] [Matt. 3:14; Mark 1:9–11; Luke 3:21–22; John 1:29–33]; at the temptation in the desert, he resisted all temptation to abuse. In the synagogue at Nazareth, he applied the prophecy of the servant of the Lord to himself [Luke 4:16–20], and from the beginning of his activity he referred to himself as the Son of Man.

This name [the Son of Man] was taken by him, as is now generally accepted, from Daniel 7:13, and demonstrates, in the first place, that Jesus took himself to be the Messiah promised in the Old Testament. In the second place, the fact that he chose this very name [the Son of Man]—avoiding the title of Messiah or king—seems to indicate that he was and wanted to be the Messiah in a different sense from how the Jews at that time generally expected their Messiah to be.[4] He did not come to set up an earthly kingdom, to be at the forefront of Israel's people, to defeat all its enemies, and raise it to the head of all nations. On the contrary, he came to serve and give his soul as a ransom for many, to seek and redeem the lost, to be delivered over and crucified, to establish in his blood a new covenant between God and man [Matt. 18:11; Mark 10:45; Luke 19:10; 22:20; 24:7; Heb. 9:15]. That is why Jesus calls himself the Son of Man every time he speaks of his humiliation.[5] In that humiliation, he sees a divine "must," a work assigned to him by the Father [18], a way he must travel to enter his glory.

It has been attempted many times to remove this divine necessity of his suffering and death, and with it the high priestly, atoning character of his death, from the original gospel. But again, without result. Not only does Jesus speak of this several times, especially near the end of his life and at the Last Supper, but the facts provide even stronger evidence [Matt. 16:21–28; 20:17–19; Mark 8:31–33; Luke 9:22–27]. Because he claimed to be the Son of God and the Messiah of Israel, he was condemned by the Sanhedrin, by the people, by Pilate; the whole life and work of Christ, according to his own word and the description of all four Gospels, ends with his death on the cross [Matt. 27:1–54; Mark 1:40; Luke 23:1–48; John 19:1–30]; and that death on the cross is the ultimate humiliation of Christ, the proof of his perfect obedience to the will of the Father, the foundation of a new covenant in his blood, the highest revelation of his and the Father's love for a sinful world, which he reconciles and preserves through it. Therefore, he could not be kept by death. On the third day, he arose from the dead and then entered into his glory [Mark 16:9; Luke 22:69; Acts 2:24, 31–32]. Jesus often calls himself the Son of Man in those places where he speaks of his future glory. Because he was the Son of God, who had a completely unique relationship with the Father and remained faithful to his will until his death on the cross, was he able to be the Messiah, the Son of Man, who entered into his glory through suffering.

This doctrine concerning the person and work of Christ, which was deliberately drawn only from the three Synoptic Gospels, in this respect, already contains in its germ everything that was later proclaimed and described by the apostles. It is true that until Christ's resurrection, the disciples did not yet have a clear understanding of his nature and work; the Gospels repeatedly make this clear [19]. That is why Jesus, in his teaching, also anticipated his young disciples' limitations, gradually trained them in the knowledge of his sonship and his messianic nature and left much to the instruction of his Spirit. But the resurrection had already brought a wonderful light to the eyes of their souls. And when, on the day of Pentecost, the exalted Christ fulfilled the promise of his Spirit to them, they not only temporarily received various extraordinary gifts of tongues and miraculous power, but they also received through that Spirit—who was the Spirit of Christ—powerful strengthening of faith, a comfort and joy such as they had not known before, a fellowship of love that bound them all together as brothers and sisters, and an extraordinary boldness to speak the word [Acts 2]. The content of that word was Christ; it gave an account of God's servant, Jesus of Nazareth, who was anointed by God with the Holy Spirit and with power [Acts 10:36–38], who was demonstrated among the Jews through powers and miracles, who went through the land doing good and healing all who were possessed by the devil and still the Jews despised and killed this Holy and Righteous One.[6] But this was done according to God's decree, according to which God has also exalted him as Lord and Christ, as Prince and Savior, who will one day return as judge of all the living and the dead, so that repentance and the forgiveness of sins may be preached in his name, for in no other is there salvation [Acts 17:31].

This was the preaching that, according to the testimony of Luke in the Acts of the Apostles, was heard especially from the lips of Peter on and after Pentecost, and it corresponds in essence to that of all the apostles. More than once, attempts have been made to point out a deep difference and a sharp contrast between the Synoptic Jesus and the Pauline or Johannine Christ, between the gospel preached by Jesus himself concerning the kingdom of God, [20] and the gospel preached by the apostles concerning Christ; and in this connection, people have sometimes gone so far as to call Paul the actual founder of (ecclesiastical) Christianity, the counterfeiter of the original gospel, even the first antichrist. But in recent years, it has become increasingly clear that it is impossible to find a different Jesus behind the Christ of Scripture; that is, one who pretended to be the Messiah, who did not perform miracles, and who did not rise from the dead. It is impossible to separate the historical Jesus and the apostolic Christ; they are one and the same person. That the historical person Jesus was the Messiah promised by God to his people in the Old Testament is the core of the Christian confession, which distinguishes it from Judaism and paganism. There is a difference in the depiction of Christ by the different apostles; there is a difference in language and style, in presentation and expression; there is also a development and expansion: the *preexistence* (*praexistence*) of Christ, his cosmic significance, his divinity, the contents and fruit of his work, and the mystical union between him and the congregation are much more clearly revealed in the Letters of Paul and in the writings of John than in the first three Gospels. But there is no contradiction;

the Synoptic Gospels are just as much testimonies of faith as all the other books of the New Testament.

Mark, whose Gospel is often held to be the oldest, begins with the significant words: "The beginning of the gospel of Jesus Christ the Son of God." All three were written at a time when the apostle Paul had already been preaching his gospel widely and had founded many congregations upon it. There is no mention of a conflict over the person and work of Christ in that first period. Paul was in complete agreement with all the apostles in this; [21] all the apostolic congregations were united in confessing that Jesus was the Christ, the Son of God, the Savior of the world, the Lord of the church, the judge of the living and the dead. They all had one Lord, one faith, one baptism; one God and Father of all, above all and in all [Eph. 4:5–7]; and one Spirit, by whom they were all built together on the foundation of the apostles and prophets into a dwelling place of God [Eph. 2:18–22].

3

THE *CONFESSION* OF CHRISTIANITY

From this confession of Jesus as the Christ began the history of doctrine. Just as the disciples of Jesus received the name of Christians in Antioch and made the impression on the outside world that they worshiped Christ as God (Plinius), so they themselves were fully conscious that they thought of Jesus Christ as God, as the judge of the living and the dead (Clement).[1] But in formulating this confession, all kinds of difficulties arose, and on the one hand they had to avoid the pitfalls of Ebionitism [a Jewish-Christian sect] and on the other hand those of Gnosticism [Docetism].[2] According to the former, Jesus was only a human being equipped with rich gifts, who was glorified and deified; and according to the latter, [Jesus was] a heavenly, divine being who temporarily appeared in the form of a human being.

Under the leadership of men like Irenaeus, Tertullian, Origen, and others, the church navigated between these two pitfalls and gradually arrived at the doctrine of the two natures whereby the Christ, being the eternal and only begotten Son of the Father, in the fullness of time from the Virgin Mary assumed human nature in unity of the person. This confession, which was pronounced at the Council of Nicaea in 325 and after many struggles was further elaborated at Chalcedon in 451, has become the confession of all Christians [22]. This teaching was not about an insignificant matter, much less about an abstract formula, but about the essence of Christianity itself, about its absolute character, about its peculiar distinctions from Judaism and paganism, about the reality and finality of the revelation of God given in Christ, and thus also about the independent existence and distinct life of the church.

In the doctrine of the two natures, whose human shortcomings need not therefore be denied, it was maintained that a two-sided consideration of Christ, according to the flesh and the spirit, from below and above, was not sufficient, that the incarnation was essentially distinct from and far superior to inspiration and inhabitation, and that Christ, as far as the flesh was concerned, was also God above all and everything, to be praised for all eternity. Around this doctrine an entire confession, extending as it were over the whole world, could now be constructed, for this Christ was the Son of the Father, who in the beginning created the world and formed mankind in his image. He was himself the mediator of the re-creation, who had objectively reconciled and reunited in his person and work the world—corrupted by sin—with God; and after his ascension, he poured out his Spirit, so that through word and sacrament, he might gather and confirm the congregation, and renew and sanctify humanity and the world into a kingdom of God.

Christianity gave birth to a special science—theology—which, resting on the baptismal formula (Matt. 28:19) and on the apostolic symbol that had certainly come into being at the beginning of the second century, had a Trinitarian character. We must therefore bear in mind that, viewed from the subjective side, Christianity is a religion, a confession of man.[3] But that confession means precisely that God as Father, Son, and [23] Spirit establishes a great work in the world and in humanity. And then, the truth and glory of Christianity becomes clear for the eyes of our soul—when we see it from the objective, theological side and listen to the hymn of faith in it—of a divine work in which the Father reconciles his created but fallen world in the death of his Son, and through his Spirit recreates it into a kingdom of God.

Then the differences between Christianity and other religions also catches the eye. The lower religions (animism, spiritism, fetishism) usually still contain the recognition of a supreme being, who is called the great Spirit, the high Father, the great Lord, etc.; but this is a dead faith, at least in the lower circles of the people: practically, their religion is absorbed in superstition and magic. The higher religions do not lack noble traits, so that they are not merely antithetical to Christianity but offer various points of reference for its mission. But they have a completely different character than the Christian religion.[4] This is most evident from the place and significance which are attributed to their founders. For example, Confucius in the Chinese religion, Gautama in the Buddhist religion, and Mohammed in the Islamic religion may have been highly gifted men who indicated a certain path to salvation, but man has to walk this path for himself and is ultimately his own savior; they are all autosoteric [self-saving].

In Christianity, however, Christ is so to speak Christianity itself;[5] he did not live once on earth only to leave his instructions and example behind, but he is the living Lord who is now seated at the right hand of God, and who continues and completes the work of re-creation. In connection with this, all the articles of faith in the religions mentioned have a different content, both about God and the [24] world, and also about man, his sin, his renewal, and his destiny. The Chinese religion is deistic, Buddhism atheistic, Islam fatalistic. In none of them is there a proper understanding of the holiness of God and the nature of sin, of the work of redemption, and the triumph of the kingdom of God. Unknown to them all is the love of the Father, the grace of the Son, and the fellowship of the Holy Spirit. And that we are able to judge all these religions in this way, from a higher point of view, to recognize the good in them and to point out the false and imperfect, we owe to Christianity, which thus proves itself to be the true religion and the standard of others.

Christianity, however, is far from being complete in its creed, in its doctrine and theology, in its world- and life-view (*wereld- en levensbeschouwing*), although these too are of great value;[6] but it is also the origin of a new, holy life. This became very clear among the first Christians and in the original churches, in spite of all their faults. A spiritual renewal had taken place within them, which was also expressed externally in all their actions and deeds and received its sign and seal in baptism. That baptism was the Jordan through which one passed from the wicked world into the kingdom of God; the ark in which one was separated from mankind that had perished in the flood and preserved for eternal life; the death of the old person and the resurrection of the new person.

By no means did conversion always have such a miraculous and sudden character as in Paul's case [Acts 9:1–9; 22:6–21; 26:21–28]. But the Jews were nonetheless released from their particularistic and legalistic viewpoint and accepted into the wider and freer circle that also honored their Messiah as the savior of the world. It could generally be testified of the Gentiles who came over to Christianity what Paul says of the Corinthians: that in former times they were [25] fornicators, idolaters, drunkards, slanderers, but that now they were cleansed, sanctified, justified in the name of the Lord Jesus and by the Spirit of our God [1 Cor. 6:9–11]. They were converted from their idols, from their idolatry, from their superstitious and immoral practices, from their whole vain walk to the living God, and they experienced that conversion as a transition from darkness to light, from fear and anxiety to the certainty and joy of faith.

In those Christians, in the midst of the Jewish and pagan world, different and new people were appearing who knew themselves to be children of God; who were proud of the forgiveness of their sins and in the hope of their glory; who distinguished themselves by their truth, honor, love, mercy, self-denial, patience, courage of faith, and many other virtues; and who did not fail, by their faithful confession and their holy lives, to make a deep impression on those who were outside. And such a power of renewal has remained inherent in Christianity throughout the ages. There are—who would dare or be able to deny it?—dark, gloomy pages in the history of the Christian church. One need only think of the shrewd and fierce doctrinal disputes, the unloving reproaches and condemnations, the inquisition and punishments for heretics, the religious wars and witch trials, the clerical world domination, and the unnatural contempt of the world, etc. But for all that, one should not overlook the comfort it has poured into our hearts, the intimate and tender piety it has cultivated, the holy life it has enabled us to attain. Churches and monasteries, charitable foundations for all kinds of poor people, evangelism and missions, family and society, architecture, painting and poetry, all the goods of our rich culture are eloquent witnesses of [Christianity]. Christianity has revealed to us the heart of God and also the heart of mankind.

[26] In the course of its history, Christianity has become more and more diverse. In drawing attention to this diversity and distinction, we must not forget the unity that is still present in all this diversity. We can rightly speak of a Christianity beneath and within the divisions of faith; the baptismal formula and the apostolic creed form the basis of all church confessions.[7] But the original fellowship of the faithful did not last long. Already in the apostolic age, all kinds of legalistic, ascetic, gnostic, and theosophical heresies began to appear; and as Christianity penetrated deeper into life and into the whole world and came into closer contact with the culture of the time, it ran the risk of losing its original purity and absorbing all kinds of foreign elements.

It should also be noted that the Greek Old Testament contained many apocryphal books, and because of this made way for all kinds of other Jewish and Greek writings: the fact that the Gospels and Epistles of the apostles had not yet been collected, and that many congregations did not know all of them and therefore did not read them in the public gatherings; that they sometimes considered writings such as those of Barnabas and Hermas worthy of the honor; and that in those days, people still lived to a great extent from tradition, which originated with the apostles but which, of course, gradually became polluted and falsified.

The first Christians were far from being able to immediately take possession of the rich content of the gospel as proclaimed by the apostles. The sharp decline in thought and spirit that can be observed in post-apostolic literature in comparison with that of the apostles provides conclusive evidence of this. They brought their origin and upbringing with them and were repeatedly influenced by those whom they had to combat. Jewish and [27] pagan ideas often penetrated their circles, legalistic and ascetic tendencies were accepted by them, and philosophical gnostic ideas were strongly sympathized with in some circles. Under these and similar influences, not only did many heresies and sects develop but also different types of Christianity, of which the Eastern or Greek and the Western or Latin types were the most important in the first centuries. In considering these two types more closely, one must not start from the idea that they, as if they were philosophical systems, must or can be derived from one principle. They are organic plants that have absorbed all kinds of ingredients, structures of which the materials have been brought together from different sides, but which have nevertheless been mixed together in such a way that they display one character and one style.

The fall of Jerusalem brought a final separation between Jews and Christians. From then on, Christianity spread almost exclusively among the Gentiles; and although Paul had penetrated further and further into the West on his missionary journeys, the center of gravity of the church still remained in the East for a long time. It was there that the most important heresies took place; it was there that the apologists emerged and after them, the true theologians; it was there that trinitarian and christological doctrine was formed. There also took place the transition from independent, free congregations—which the New Testament introduces to us—to the one, all-encompassing congregation—the hierarchically structured

Catholic Church—in which the bishops as the successors of the apostles are the keepers of tradition, the teachers of the people, the ministers of sacrifice, the dispensers of mysteries [28].

There also arose that type of Christianity which is usually referred to as Eastern or Greek, and which can be briefly described as follows. While the Logos had already had an illuminating effect on the world before his incarnation, he revealed knowledge and life primarily through his incarnation and resurrection. Since the consequences of the fall consisted particularly in humans yielding to their sensual desires and consequently to destruction and death, they needed these two benefits above all: the knowledge of spiritual and eternal things, and an imperishable, blessed life. Man acquires this knowledge through faith, which man with his freedom of will—impaired by sin, but not lost—is capable of and that consists solely in a rational acceptance of orthodox truths purely preserved by the church, especially in the doctrines of the Trinity and the incarnation. The Greek Church is the church of orthodoxy, which wants to stand its ground unchanged with the theology of the church fathers up to Damascene, and which since February 19 of 842, the day when Empress Theodora returned the statues to the churches of Constantinople, has annually celebrated the Feast of Orthodoxy on the same date. So much is this adherence to ancient tradition a characteristic of Eastern Christianity that the Russian Church still follows the Julian calendar, begins the week with Monday and each day at six o'clock in the morning. Even the state is subservient to the maintenance of orthodoxy. From the beginning, the church in the East closely aligned herself with the world power, which was given its seat in Byzantium through Constantine, and has remained faithful to it [the world power] in Russia to this day. It does not know the ideal of one catholic church encompassing the whole of Christendom as Rome does; it is content to be a second church next to Rome; it even consists [29] at present of no less than sixteen autocephalous (individual) churches, which together number about one hundred million Christians, of which the Russian Church with its eighty-five million members is the most important. This Russian Church venerates the czar as the guardian of orthodoxy, the protector of the faith, who maintains the religious unity of the people through all kinds of coercive measures, and who must violently suppress and banish Judaism as well as numerous sects.[8]

But orthodox doctrine, of which the Eastern Church boasts, is not the source of its religious life. The mysteries of the Trinity and the incarnation may be an appropriate object of theological speculation, including everything connected with the practice of deep veneration; but [these mysteries] remain high above the masses and are deemed irrelevant for religious life, which [the Eastern Church] nourishes from other sources. Greek theologians consider it a privilege of their church that their religious life is not based so much on ideas as on feelings. Although the laity accept the [church's] teaching and hear reading and preaching from the Scriptures, they base their [spiritual lives] on something else—the mystical cult (*mystieken cultus*) on which their whole church and household worship are organized.[9] In various [orthodox] churches, which are similarly uniform, their wall of icons is of great importance, as it separates the altar space intended for priests (with its associated rooms) from the space allocated to laypeople; and in homes, a saint's icon with a burning candle sits in the center of a room. The religious life of the devout—especially of the clergy, monks, and nuns—is absorbed in veneration of the saints, icons and relics, fasting and prayers; everything connected with the church and cult is deeply venerated; and the sacraments are more high and holy mysteries than they are *means of grace* (*vehicula gratiæ*). [30] Orthodoxy and mysticism, doctrine and life stand more or less dualistically side by side. This dualism has found its theological expression in their rejection of the *filioque*: that in the divine being, the Holy Spirit does not proceed from the Son, but only from the

Father. In order, the Son and the Spirit are not after, but next to each other; they both have their origin and principle only in the Father, who is the source of the Godhead and who reveals himself in both; while the Son makes the Father knowable, it is the Spirit who makes him encounterable.

In the West, Christianity developed in a very different direction. However, one should beware of exaggeration and not seek contrast where there is none. The Western and Eastern churches had, and still possess, much in common. The doctrine of the Trinity and the Christology of the East were generally accepted in the West; the struggle of Augustine and Pelagius had little influence in the East, but the East took sides against Pelagius and for Augustine. In the Middle Ages, the doctrine of the seven sacraments as well as transubstantiation was largely adopted by the East. Rome sees the Eastern churches not as primarily heretical but as schismatic churches with which it would like to reunite. Whether this will happen any time soon is doubtful. The difference concerns not only a few more or less significant doctrines (*filioque*, sprinkling, unleavened bread in the sacrament, the refusal of the chalice, celibacy of priests, purgatory, indulgences, immaculate conception of Mary, and the infallibility of the pope), but it also consists of a different vision of Christianity. Just compare Origen with Tertullian, or Athanasius with Augustine, to get a deeper impression. In the East, the philosophical, intellectual spirit of the Greeks was at work; while in the West, the judicial, analytical, [31] and organizing spirit of Rome was at work. There [in the East], theological and christological doctrines were and remained on the agenda for centuries; here [in the West], thinking was primarily occupied with anthropological and soteriological doctrines throughout the centuries—that is, before Augustine, during his time, and then after him. The Greek Church sees sin primarily as separation from God, it emphasizes the incarnation and resurrection of Christ and the unity of the two natures, and it considers the primary act of salvation to lie in living in fellowship with God. The Latin Church [Rome] sees sin primarily in terms of its guilt and punishment; and when considering the person of Christ, it keeps a sharp eye on the distinction between the two natures, it looks for the value of his work particularly in his voluntary suffering and death, and it sees the forgiveness of sins, the deliverance from guilt and punishment, as the most important benefit of salvation. Although the two are in many ways opposed, Rome in a certain sense prepared the way for the Reformation. There was no place for it in the East.

According to Rome, God created man immediately in his "image," but not immediately in his "likeness." With the image alone, man was still only a *natural man* (*homo naturalis*) belonging to and destined for this earth. If he had remained in that condition, he might have been able to naturally do good works and thus acquire earthly bliss and glory, but he would never be admitted to heaven and never into the immediate presence of God. However, since God—according to his will—wished to raise man to this supernatural heavenly glory, he was compelled to equip him [32] not only with his image but also with his likeness. This likeness consists of a *superadded gift* (*donum superadditum*), which was added to *natural man* (*homo naturalis*) (in a logical, or at a later temporal point of time) and enabled him to do supernaturally good works and thus earn supernatural, heavenly salvation: that is, the *vision of God* (*visio*) and the *enjoyment of the essence of God* (*fruitio Dei per essentiam*). Through the fall, however, man lost this supernatural addition and his natural strength was also more or less weakened, yet not enough to prevent him from doing naturally good works. But even if he could do them all and perfectly, he would only be able to obtain earthly, never heavenly, salvation.[10] Therefore, grace is essential. In the first place, in an absolute sense, this grace is necessary to lift up the natural man who is deprived of the supernatural addition to the supernatural state again ([*elevating grace*] *gratia elevans*). Only in the second place is it coincidentally necessary to repair the lesser or greater damage which sin has inflicted on his nature ([*healing grace*] *gratia sanans*).

This grace has now been acquired in all its fullness by Christ, especially through the profound humiliation to which he submitted himself in his incarnation and throughout his life, but in particular in his suffering and death. He was not obliged to undergo this humiliation, this absolute *humiliation* (*humilitas*) either as a God or as a man; it was entirely voluntary, not a precept, but a *counsel* (*consilium*), a *superfluous good work* (*opus supererogatorium*) of infinite value, because it was the work of the God-man and consisted in absolute self-denial and total commitment to God's will. Christ was *the* sufferer extraordinaire, the divine martyr, whose passive obedience had such an infinite merit that even a [33] single drop of blood would have been sufficient for the redemption of the entire human race because of his union with the divine nature.

[Rome believes that] Christ has now entrusted all this superabundant grace (and truth) to his church for distribution. In [the church], he himself lives on earth: it is the continuation of his incarnation; in the mass, he repeats in an unbloody manner his sacrifice on the cross; through the priest, he communicates his grace in the sacrament; through the infallible mouth of the pope, he leads his church in the truth. The church is therefore first and foremost an institution of salvation, not an assembly of believers or a community of saints, but a supernatural institution established by God to preserve and distribute the saving grace and truth here on earth. Whatever is lacking in the doctrine and life of the faithful, the church remains the same in spite of it, for it has its center in the priesthood and sacrament, and therein always shares the characteristics of unity and holiness, of catholicity, and apostolicity.

Therefore, the distinction between clergy and laity is necessary and intrinsic to the church as a whole. There is a "teaching church," which possesses and distributes the goods of salvation, and a "hearing church," which receives and enjoys them, a distinction that is expressed in the church building with the separation of the choir and the nave, and which gradually transforms the table of the faithful into the altar of the priest. Among these clergy, the bishop is the central figure, because he has descended from the apostles in unbroken succession. He is in possession of tradition and, above all, has *the power to propagate the priesthood* (*vis generativa sacerdotii*), which means the power of (or "coming from") the sacrament of ordination to increase the priesthood and thus the church itself, from generation to generation. Below him are the lower offices (acolytes or ministers, exorcists, readers, and [34] doorkeepers or sextons), in addition to the presbyter and deacon, who are his auxiliaries and organs; and upwards the episcopate, through the ranks of archbishop, metropolitan and patriarch, attains its unity and conclusion in the pope, who is not only bishop of Rome but, as the successor of Peter, is also *first* (*primas*) in the entire church and representative of Christ.

Only in dependence on and in communion with the pope can the other members of the clergy have and exercise their power. This power is of two kinds: a *power of order* (*potestas ordinis*), which gives them authority to perform religious acts and to distribute the means of grace; and a *power of jurisdication* (*potestas jurisdictionis*), which is included in the office itself or is given by a specific commission, to govern the church. This whole power is not thought of as a serving one, but as a governing one—as a real governmental power with legislative, judicial, and executive rights. The doctrine, proclaimed with infallibility by the pope *from the episcopal seat* (*ex cathedra*), has the same character as the laws of the state; while the grace dispensed by the priest in the sacrament is a collapse of divine power which raises natural man to a higher order and enables him to do supernaturally good works.

Word and faith have a subordinate, preparatory significance; it is the sacrament which *by virtue of the work performed* (*ex opere operato*) communicates grace to everyone who does not place a proper obstacle in the way, and this in such a way that each sacrament confers a special grace. Baptism restores the supernatural addition lost through sin, takes away all guilt and blemish of past sins, and incorporates the believer into the community. Among this group, confirmation separates the strong from the weak and makes them soldiers under Christ as king. Ordination [35] separates the priests from the laity and elevates them to the likeness of Christ as high priest.

These three sacraments thus incorporate a different hierarchical status and therefore leave a mark that is never erased. The other four sacraments—communion, marriage, penance, and last rites—serve in general to reinforce the received grace and enable one to pursue and reach the goal that each sacrament particularly has in view. Especially in the sacrament of penance does the magistral and judicial character of the church according to Rome become clear. For although the believer is completely freed in baptism from all guilt and blemish of sin, the natural lust of the flesh remains; and although this is not a sin in itself, it is often easily an occasion for sin. The sins committed in this way by the baptized person must be confessed in the confessional before the priest, especially when they are mortal sins that cause the received grace to be completely lost. This [priest] sits as a judge, who—following the confessor's complete and utter confession—must inform them of the number and nature of the sins committed. [The priest] may refuse or distribute absolution (the forgiveness of guilt and the eternal punishment of sins), and in the latter case may bind them with the prescription of certain good works (prayers, fasts, alms, etc.), to pay off the temporary punishments that are inseparable from sins here or in purgatory.

When the believer has received supernatural grace from the priest in the sacrament in this manner, he may do good works that arise from a supernatural power and are also, according to merit, worthy of supernatural salvation. [According to Rome, then,] grace actually only serves to put humanity back to work [36] and make them capable of achieving their aims. It is not a restoration of God's favor but a divine power, a supernatural quality in mankind, that can make man regain that favor through good works. Therefore, for the believer, everything comes down to the proper use of the received power of grace. But, of course, this involves all kinds of differences in effort, desire, and zeal.

There is one road to heavenly salvation, but all do not walk at the same speed and all do not exert themselves to the same degree. There are commandments in the Christian moral teaching which everyone must observe, but there are also suggestions which can be freely followed or not. When someone sacrifices and chastises himself more, withdraws from the world, and especially observes the voluntary vows of chastity, poverty, and obedience, he does not reach a higher perfection, but he reaches that perfection—which is destined for all believers—in a faster and safer manner with less danger of temptation. Therefore, devoting oneself to a profession or business, to life in the family, society, and the state, or cultural work in general, according to Rome, this is not sinful in itself, but it does carry with it many dangers of deviation, stagnation, and regression in grace.

After all, these fields are of a lesser order; they act on man's desires and are actually controlled by evil spirits and the devil. The church alone can break this power of temptation, and it does so in the most varied ways: through its sacraments and sacramentals, through holy acts (blessings, ordinations, incantations), and through holy things (amulets, phylacteries, scapulars, etc.); as long as the natural is not consecrated by the church, it remains profane and of inferior rank. The same principle which gave rise to worldly contempt also gave birth to [37] world domination and is also the cause of the so-called double standard. This in turn led further to the doctrine of the transferability of merits, whereby the deficiency of one person can be made up for by the excess of another. The martyrs, the monks, the nuns, the saints in a special sense, the *faithful of highest quality* (*religiosi par excellence*) who devote their whole lives to God, whose life is a single devotion, not only accomplish what they owe, but they may also do superfluous good works, the merits of which increase the spiritual treasure of the church.

Out of this treasure, the church—by prayers, alms, the sacrifice of the mass, and especially by means of indulgences—can mitigate or shorten the temporary punishments which the other faithful here or in purgatory still have to bear for their sins. Yet whatever and however many graces the church extends to its children through all these avenues, it never gives them the certainty of salvation; it always mixes hope and fear on their behalf, as Gregory the Great said.[11] A few may have received such a guarantee through special revelation, and a few others may be declared holy and blessed by the pope; yet the majority of believers arrive in purgatory after death for a time—shorter or longer nobody can determine—not to be purified, but to pay the temporary punishments they still owe.

The diversity here on earth corresponds to the diversity in the afterlife. The faithful of the Old Testament went to a place in the underworld upon their death, from which they were first delivered by Christ; the unbaptized and the children who died early descend into their destined afterlife; and in heaven, a distinction also remains among the blessed: for while all receive the "golden crown," some who have led a particularly holy life [38] are given "golden wreaths." All, like the angels, share the same holiness and blessedness, but not all to the same degree. Like the angels, the blessed in heaven even now form a spiritual hierarchy. At the top is Mary and after her follow the patriarchs, the prophets, the apostles, the martyrs, etc., in an ever-descending series. The closer someone is to God and shares his nature, the higher his rank and the more he is an object of veneration for the faithful on earth. Therefore, in this too there are all kinds of difference. There is *worship which belongs to God alone* (*latria*), and of which the human nature of Christ and all its members (e.g. the sacred heart) is an object, although not for the sake of worshiping God alone. The saints and everything associated with the saints (vestments, houses, tombs, relics), on account of sharing in the scent of their holiness, are entitled to ordinary *veneration* (*dulia*) and relative veneration; but above all, Mary is entitled to *more than ordinary veneration* (*hyperdulia*). There are as many kinds of worship as there are degrees of excellence. Hierarchical, monarchical order is the basic idea that governs Rome's doctrine of the angels and the blessed, of the world and the church, of the laity and the clergy, of worship and art.

4

THE *DIVERSITY* OF CHRISTIANITY

The deeper one thinks about the firmness and power of Roman Christianity, the greater the admiration one feels for the German Reformer who initially dared to act alone against this system and who persevered in this resistance to the end. Many people before and after Luther rebelled against Rome, but they were either violently suppressed or they recanted and laid their heads in their laps. Luther, however, stood his ground; the words he spoke in [39] Worms "Here I stand, I cannot do otherwise, God help me" may not be above suspicion historically, but they are a striking expression of the spirit that animated him and enabled him to fight. The Roman Church bound eternal salvation to its fellowship and burdened with a curse anyone who turned their back on it and was no longer served by its mediation. But Luther had the courage to resist [the Roman church] because he had experienced a certainty of salvation in believing in God's grace in Christ, which made the church's claim to salvation superfluous in his eyes.

The Reformation had its origin not in intellectual reasoning, or in a well-considered decision of the will, but in a religious-ethical experience. It had already been prepared in Luther's heart long before it became a historical fact when he posted his Ninety-Five Theses at the Wittenberg Castle Chapel on October 31, 1517. Research conducted in recent years—especially Luther's comments on Lombard's *Sententiae* in 1509/10, his readings on the Psalms in 1513/15 and on Paul's letters to the Romans in 1515/16—have raised no doubts. The light dawned on him as early as perhaps 1512 when he gained new insight into the nature of God's righteousness, of which Paul speaks in Romans 1:17, and he came to know it as a righteousness that does not demand a penalty and punishment but rather gives and graciously forgives.[1]

Gradually, he was led further onward from this new point of view. Even before his public appearance, he began to criticize in the pulpit and the lectern many abuses that had gradually crept into the church, and he urged reform of theological studies, especially in the Ninety-Five Theses of Sept. 4, 1517.[2] The first conflict [40] arose with Tetzel's trade in indulgences, whereby the remission of temporary punishments, whether here or in purgatory, was made available in exchange for money and the papal treasury obtained a large profit. When Luther heard about this trade near Wittenberg, his mind was stirred, which prompted him to write [his] Ninety-Five Theses. Yet he did not insist on abolition in any way but only on the restriction and purification of indulgences. In fact, he did not conflict with any doctrine but only with the practice of the church; he stood up for the honor of the church against its entrenched abuses. Nevertheless, a trial was soon started against him, which lasted no less than three years. It ended with a papal ban signed by the pope on June 15, 1520, which Luther publicly burned in Wittenberg on December 12 along with other papal decrees. With this, the fellowship [with Rome] was broken and Protestantism was forced to go its own way and conquer its own sphere.

The name Protestantism—by which later on all churches and movements are summarized, which directly or indirectly originated from the Reformation—is derived from the historical circumstance of the protest, which was lodged by the evangelical princes and cities at the Reichstag at Speyer in 1529 against the decision of the majority to leave the Roman religion unrestricted in their area for the time being and thereby to halt the progress of the Reformation.[3] Already for that reason [the name Protestant] is unsuitable to inform us about the principle and character of the Reformation. In addition, it possesses such a general and vague meaning that it is useless for investigating the nature of Protestantism; it could end up as nothing more than an abstract phrase where each direction [41] thinks its own way.

On the other hand, the principle from which Luther's reformation activities arose can be clearly indicated and described. He himself was converted at a time when he learned through "divine illumination" to understand Paul's meaning and view of God's righteousness. The question is not whether Luther presented a new and previously unknown interpretation of this expression in Romans 1:17, for [Heinrich] Denifle has irrefutably demonstrated the opposite.[4] But Roman piety, according to both doctrine and practice, always bore this quality: that man, through the grace received at baptism, was enabled to make himself worthy of the community of God and eternal salvation through supernatural good works. Sanctification preceded justification, man's work preceded God's favor, merit preceded reward, and ethics preceded religion.

On the other hand, Luther learned from experience that this road does not lead to salvation and security and that the gospel, as it appears in the New Testament and especially in Paul's words, takes a completely different road. For in that gospel, God was the first to bestow of mere grace upon mankind in Christ, to receive him into his fellowship, and to share in his fatherly favor; and man on his part could only accept that rich gift with a childlike, thankful faith. In this way, the whole relationship was fundamentally and dramatically reversed: God again assumed the position before man, his undeserved gift before man's actions, faith before works, and religion before ethics.

The transformation that man underwent in his relationship to God through that faith naturally also brought about a change in his inner disposition. For he came to know God, whom he formerly had feared as a wrathful judge, now as [42] a merciful Father, who had freely forgiven him all his sins and had received his favor and fellowship without any merit on his part; where his heart had hitherto been sorrowful to death and had trembled and shuddered under the shadow of God's wrath, it now learned to revel in undeserved forgiveness and rejoiced in salvation and joy; and its will, which had always regarded and feared the good work as a slave's work for gain, now received an inner yearning to do good work out of love and gratitude, because it was the will of his Father in heaven. The difference between the Reformation and Rome was therefore not fundamentally about whether justification was juridical or ethical, as it was later formulated, but about whether justification, consisting of both, changed the relationship to God and the inner disposition of the heart that was effected by God's grace or by man's work, by prior gift or by subsequent reward, by faith alone or also by works, by God descending to man or by man attempting to ascend to God.

From this basic idea, Luther continued on his path and came into conflict with Rome more severely and on increasingly more points. But again, that did not happen according to a predetermined plan. As at its inception, the Reformation was not a work of rational calculation. Especially not so with Luther, who did not have a logical and systematic mind, nor did he excel in organizing his books and pamphlets, several hundred in number; they are nearly all incidental writings. What was lacking in himself, he admired in [Philip] Melanchthon, who was the first to bring unity and order to the chaos of Reformation thinking.

Luther was not a man of discursive [43] thinking but of intuition; a man of spirit and ingenuity, of strength and courage, of will and deed; not of a constructive but of a creative nature, more a father than a teacher of the church.[5] In his teaching and in his work, as well as in his person and in his character, he combined elements that are irreconcilable. But the principle of justification by faith, which he had discovered as the core of the gospel, nevertheless led him to a number of conclusions, three of which are more noteworthy than others.

First, it led him to recognize the authority of Scripture, as opposed to the authority of church and tradition, and to value the various parts of Scripture in proportion to the degree to which they *"urge Christ"* (*treiben Christum*); that which he had experienced within his soul, the contrast between justification by works and justification by faith, came to be seen objectively in his consciousness as a contrast between the church, which preached the former, and Scripture, which testified to the latter.

Second, this led him to a different understanding of the church, priesthood, and sacrament. If Scripture alone had authority, the church would assume second place and be subordinate to the word. The Reformers did not think of rejecting the church itself or of founding a completely new order outside it; they remained with both feet within Christianity and within the church; they held fast to its continuity and even adopted the confessions of the first four councils. They continued to regard the Trinity, the incarnation, and satisfaction as the fundamental doctrines of the Christian faith; but within those limits they tried, according to the rule of God's word, to purify Christianity and the church again from the errors and abuses which had crept in. The church had to become again what she ought to be according to her idea. In comparison, it did not consist of priesthood and sacrament but of the fellowship [44] of the faithful themselves, who were the people of God, the body of Christ, the temple of the Holy Spirit, all anointed as prophets and priests. Before the church became an institution, it was already an organism, which receives its life from Christ as its head, and which with its organization, government, and worship can have no other purpose than to bring the word of Christ to full authority in its confession and life.

And third, from the principle of the Reformation flowed a significant change in religious and moral life. Where there is forgiveness, there is life and salvation, according to Luther's word.

Religion can then no longer consist in the observance of all kinds of duties, in the veneration of saints, images, and relics, in vigils and fasts, or in almsgiving and pilgrimages, as if we were doing God a service and had to gain his favor by this. True, genuine religion consists in the fact that:

> I, as dear as the salvation of my soul is to me, I shun and flee away from all idolatry, sorcery, divination or superstition, invocation of the saints or other creatures, and only get to know the one true God, to only trust in him, to subject myself to him alone in all humility and patience, to expect all good things from him alone, to love, fear and honor him with all my heart, and to rather depart from all creatures and forsake them than that I do something in the least against his will. [Heidelberg Catechism Answer 94 to Question 94: "What does God enjoin in the first commandment?"]

This indeterminate trust in God gives also the moral life its origin and strength. True conversion lasts throughout life and consists in the death of the old and the resurrection of the new, in fleeing from sin and in living according to God's will. Good works are not slave-like services which we perform out of fear of God and hope of reward, and they consist not in all kinds of abstinence and self-torture, founded on human ordinances; but they are the fruits of faith, and their standard is found in [45] God's will, and they have his honor as their goal. They are not practiced outside of the world but in the midst of life in society; their territory is the family, earthly profession, the work of culture, and the love of brethren and neighbors. The negative, ascetic relationship in which the pious had found himself with the world before was transformed into a positive one in the Reformation: it turned the face of the Christian toward nature and the culture around him and pointed him there to his sphere of action. Every honest profession was a calling of God and a service to the community.

In these basic ideas, there was great harmony among the Reformers. But soon differences appeared among them. Although

[Ulrich] Zwingli held Luther in high esteem, he did not agree with his sacramental doctrine. This difference was not settled at a conference in Marburg in 1529 but later; despite the mediation efforts of [John] Calvin, it continued to worsen and led to an irreparable split on the Lutheran side, which was led in particular by [Tilemann] Heshusius, about 1560.

The profound difference in character between the German and Swiss Reformations first became clear in the struggle over the Lord's Supper. According to repeated investigations after the introduction of the Union in 1817, [these differences] are tied to all kinds of psychological and historical, national and political, geographic and economic peculiarities that existed from the beginning. It is therefore difficult to summarize it in a single formula and to reduce it to an abstract principle. But everyone feels that church and theology, that piety and life between the Lutherans and the Reformed, exhibits a different character.

Luther came to the comforting realization of God's [46] forgiving grace in Christ through a fearful soul's experience of sinfulness and fear of God's wrath. Penitence as *repentance* (*poenitentia*), as fear and dread wrought by the law, preceded faith. Luther did not think of prescribing his experience to others as a rule. But the view that the law was primarily of significance to the unconverted, condemning them and driving them toward Christ, permeated all of his followers and left its mark on Luther's theology.

On the other hand, of course, in the gospel the emphasis was already on the blessing of justification; all of the church depended on this article. In the consciousness of the gracious forgiveness of all his sins, the Christian felt completely comforted and blessed; he lived in and enjoyed the consciousness that he had received a gracious God. This gives Lutheran piety a character of freedom and joy, which often found eloquent expression in song. But it also meant that there was no need to trace this religious life back to God's election, or to confirm and seal it with good works.

Luther, like Zwingli and Calvin, did profess predestination in the beginning, but later he pushed it aside without ever revoking it. Melanchthon weakened it, and later Lutheran theology maintained it only in the Remonstrant sense. And in the same way, moral life, especially social and political life, did not come into its own. Luther had stated as strongly as possible that justification was both a change in one's relationship to and attitude toward God, and that faith was at the same time a receiving of God's grace and a renewing of mankind; but he related the moral life, which resulted from faith, only very loosely and, in fact, unwillingly to the law. The [47] dominant idea was that the Christian was free from the law and no longer had anything to do with it, that he produced good works by faith, just as the sun sends forth its rays and the flower spreads its fragrance. It is related to this that the Lutheran church and theology gradually began to place all their honor in the treasure of pure teachings; that the church could be described by Melanchthon as *the assembly of scholars* (*coetus scholasticus*), divided into those who *learn* (*docents*) and those who *hear* (*auditores*). This church could be content as long as it possessed complete freedom to preach the gospel and could leave everything else—government, discipline, care for the poor, education—to the government, and that life therefore broke down into two *hemispheres* (*hemisphaeria*), which had little to do with each other.

Zwingli and Calvin were indeed men of a different spirit, and they were brought by a different path to conversion and to the work of reform. Neither of them had the same experience of the condemning power of God's law as Luther. Zwingli, a free Swiss man and a devout student of humanism, felt all the constriction and torment of Roman superstitions, ceremonies, and commandments. He considered himself enlarged and enlightened when he learned the gospel, in which no word was dearer to him than Jesus' invitation: "Come to me, all you who are weary and burdened, and I will give you rest" [Matt. 11:28]. And Calvin, the educated Frenchman who had studied literature and law for a long time, experienced his conversion as a deliverance from error to truth, from doubt to certainty. For them, the law was not seen in the one-sided light in which Luther saw it, and consequently, although justification was a very important benefit, it was not the only benefit of the gospel. Calvin even [48] distinguished emphatically between *penitence* (*poenitentia*), fear and anxiety, which could precede but did not necessarily lead to spiritual life, and *repentance* (*resipiscentia*), true conversion, which resulted from faith, continued throughout life, and consisted in the death of the old man and the resurrection of the new. And that faith arose again from the promise of the covenant of grace, to which Calvin returned with Zwingli over against the Anabaptists and which included not only adult, believing parents but also their children from the time of conception and birth. Therefore, while maintaining the distinction, there was also a connection between nature and grace, between God's providence and redemption, between the work of the Father and that of the Son.

In the same way, the life of faith stretched forward and connected the Christian with the whole world. Justification did not stand alone for Calvin but reached out to election on the one hand and to sanctification on the other. For him, faith is not only a hand that receives but also acts; a firm and indisputable assurance, which acts and drives to action; the principle of a new life, which manifests itself in piety toward God, in moderation toward oneself, and in righteousness toward one's neighbor. Hence, Calvin was not satisfied with merely a religious reformation or with a restoration of the pure preaching of the gospel; his vision reached further and penetrated deeper. Less medieval than Luther, he also felt the weight of social and political interests. Everything had to be regulated again according to God's law and directed to his honor.

The church, an institution of Christ, not only had to guard the right ministry of the word, but also had to behave according to his command [49] in its organization, government, and discipline and to maintain and defend its independence from the authorities. The state, although distinct from the church and entrusted with its own task, was nevertheless no less bound by the word of God than the church and obliged to keep the two tablets of God's law. All domestic, civil, and social life had to submit to the discipline of God's word, which was not only found in the gospel but also in the law, and not only in the New Testament but also in the Old. Just as there is nothing in nature in which a glimmer of God's majesty does not shine, so too should the whole of human society be a mirror of his glory. All things are from God; therefore, they must all be to him. Calvin took a theological and theocentric position in contrast to Luther's anthropological and soteriological position. [Calvin's] opposition was not only directed against all Judaic works-based holiness, but also against all pagan idolatry. In principle, asceticism belongs on Roman soil; Pietism can appeal to Luther, but Puritanism is a brainchild of Calvin.[6]

5

THE *RISE OF MODERNITY* AND CHRISTIANITY

With the Reformation, we usually think only of that spiritual movement that had a firm footing in the Lutheran and Reformed churches. But this movement soon found itself limited and opposed from both the left and the right by two movements, Socinianism and Anabaptism, which, although showing some affinities with the Reformation, actually both still lived out of the medieval opposition of nature and grace, and each elaborated on this in its own way.

Socinianism interpreted [nature and grace] so sharply that it declared material to be eternal, it judged man by nature to be deprived of all knowledge of God, and it considered him to be subject to death [50] according to his soul. It was only through a supernatural revelation that knowledge of God, of his will and commandment, could be imparted to [man] and, accordingly, the way opened for him to partake of eternal life through obedience. Christ, in the same way, by supernatural conception and repeated ascension to heaven, had achieved that knowledge of God; and furthermore, by virtue of his resurrection, had entered eternal life in perfect obedience, becoming to us an example and a guarantee. Socinianism thus gave birth to an aristocratic society, to an elite elevated above ordinary people, who through knowledge and the practice of God's will, in distinction to others, obtained immortality.

Anabaptism started from the same contradiction [between nature and grace] but applied it in a democratic direction: the faithful, who had consciously been converted and had been baptized by free and explicit choice, were to flee the world and the church that had been totally corrupted by it, to withdraw from all culture, and to live independently as a cloistered congregation that would within its own circle realize the kingdom of God, if necessary by force and violence; or alternatively, they would have to patiently await the day that Christ himself would come and establish his kingdom on earth.

Both movements did no small damage to the Reformation, but even greater damage was done by the Roman Church, who with admirable energy managed to lift itself out of its decline. At the Council of Trent, she took a firm stand against the Reformation on all the most important points; in principle she conceded nothing and remained completely in agreement with herself. But still, she undertook with seriousness the reformation of the lives of clergy, monks, and laymen; by returning to scholasticism, she managed to arm herself scientifically against all attacks to which her doctrine, government, and service had been [51] exposed. Through the Order of the Jesuits, she succeeded in regaining in many countries a large part of the ground lost to the Reformation; and through missions, she extended her territory in America, India, Japan, and China. The Reformers had expected that Rome's power would weaken and wither away, but history has shown otherwise. Romanism and Protestantism continued to exist side by side, and the Reformation became an incentive for Rome to revise itself and a means toward its own recovery.

All these religious movements are important in their own right, but they are nevertheless only a part of the one powerful spiritual current that has emerged since the Crusades and led to the new era. The Middle Ages were characterized by the fact that the church was the center of all life and left its mark on all culture. There was one church, one Christianity, one pope, and one emperor, one language, science, and art. But this unity gradually came to be felt as a stranglehold; everywhere there was a noticeable effort to escape this pressure; everything began to move in the direction of freedom and independence, of emancipation and secularization. Society underwent a major change as the feudal system was broken down, the power of the nobility was reduced, and a free civilian class was created. Politically, the people withdrew more and more from the tutelage of the church, they became aware of their nationality, and restrained the arbitrariness of the rulers through their states or cities. Geographically, with the discovery of South Africa, America, and the Indies, the circle of vision expanded to all sides, and navigation, trade, and industry entered a new era of development. In philosophy, medieval scholasticism was abandoned, and at first some went back in search of Plato and [52] Aristotle, Zeno, and Epicurus; and then with [Francis] Bacon and [René] Descartes, others went on to follow their own path. In art and literature, they turned away from Gothic style and sought to connect with classical antiquity, in order to redeem man from savagery and raise him as an independent and free being.

All of these factors contributed to shaping the new era and continue to have some effect to this day. The churches could not stop these emerging forces and knew even less how to direct them. They clung to their doctrinal system, becoming increasingly distanced from life, and entered the grave period of orthodoxy not long before the middle of the seventeenth century. Naturally, there was a reaction against this; the seventeenth century was characterized, especially in its latter half, by the awakening of the subject who, unsatisfied by church and theology, sought satisfaction in other ways.

Even within the Roman Church, a parallel direction can be discerned. Not only were many new congregations formed (for the veneration of the Sacred Heart of Jesus by Marguerite Alacoque, etc.), but Gallicanism, Quietism, and Jansenism each in their own way fought against the Roman system. However, much stronger was the reaction in the Protestant churches. When one needs convincing, one only has to think of Precicism, Biblicism, Cocceianism, and Labadism in the Netherlands, the Saumur School in France, Puritanism, Independentism, Baptism, Quakerism in England, and Pietism, Syncretism, Moravianism in Germany, etc.

The sight of the tremendous divisions and ruptures to which the churches were prey awakened the desire of many to go behind [their] differences, back to a common confession, and to restore therein [their] broken unity. While some [53] thought they could find a common confession in the first councils, in the apostolic symbol, or in the Holy Scriptures, Deism in England took the most radical approach. It took its standpoint in the natural religion and morality innate in all men, and it sought from that standpoint to demonstrate by philosophical grounds that all supernatural revelation was impossible, unnecessary, and unknowable, and to show through critical arguments that the Bible did not intend to teach such supernatural revelation but had essentially only natural religion as its object.

In the self-indulgent eighteenth century, people also thought they had no need for anything at all besides God, virtue, and immortality. At creation, God had equipped both the world and man, his mind and will, with sufficient powers to be able to save himself and work out his own perfection and salvation. These ideas found fertile soil on the continent of Europe, prepared by Pietism and Rationalism; they were propagated in France by the encyclopedists, in Germany by the men of the Enlightenment (*Aufklärung*), and they brought about a total change in the way Christianity was viewed, though not so much by the masses as by cultured society. This change was indeed so radical that one cannot help but speak of the birth of a new Protestantism.

Until now, some doctrines had been contested, but the foundations of Christianity had been left intact. Now the supernatural foundation itself was undermined, and Christianity was completely deprived of its peculiar character. [Christianity] was in its essence as old as creation and—insofar as it appeared in a historical, pictorial form—merely the embodiment of eternal truths of reason that man already possessed in his common sense or at least could have [54] discovered for himself. In principle, therefore, this Rationalism differed from the Reformation, which did not start from abstract reason but began from a religious-ethical experience, which was awakened in the soul of its leaders in response to the Holy Scriptures. On the other hand, the Rationalism of the eighteenth century shows many traits of affinity with Humanism and Socinianism, with the understanding, however, that it had at its disposal weapons that were unknown in the sixteenth century and were furnished by the newer natural science and philosophy.

6

THE *RESPITE* OF CHRISTIANITY

The struggle that Deism and Rationalism undertook against Christianity in the eighteenth century was carried out in an even more radical way in the nineteenth century. The character of this century cannot be described in a single brief formula; it is far too complex for that. One can search for its distinguishing features equally in the awakening of the historical as in that of the physical science, in the expansion of transportation as in the development of technology, in the yearning for emancipation as in the rise of democracy. But this is certain: that the aversion to supernaturalism has been inherent in it to a great extent, and that the whole of modern culture is geared toward only taking account of immanent forces and laws. Philosophy, physics, and history alike have worked in this direction. The inductive method, causality, which gradually gained the upper hand, was noticed everywhere in phenomena, and the idea of evolution, which consciously or unconsciously served as the guiding principle in all research, have narrowed the supernaturalistic world- and life-view (*wereld- en levensbeschouwing*) of Christianity to such an extent that there seemed to be no room left for it.

How long and how broad are the attacks undertaken against Christianity and the accusations leveled [55] against it! [It is said:] the Scriptures of the Old and New Testaments are false, forged, unreliable, and do not in the least give a true picture of the history of Israel, or of the origin and earliest essence of Christianity; the life of Jesus is so obscured that nothing can be said with certainty; he may well have existed as a historical person, who was later idealized and deified by the congregation, but it is also possible that he was entirely a product of religious fantasy; the church, which is named after him, is built on an error—namely, the belief in his resurrection, and throughout its history, both as regards its doctrine and its organization and service, has been one great aberration; instead of being a blessing, it has been a curse for mankind through its divisions and disputes, through its persecutions and heretical trials, through its suppression of all freedom and its opposition to all culture; its creed and doctrine are totally worthless and in every respect in conflict with the results of science; even Christian ethics and philanthropy are out of date and no longer fit for application in our social and political relations. In a word, Christianity has had its time, we have outgrown it completely, and we are, insofar as we are modern cultural people, no longer Christians.

The crisis in which Christianity finds itself today as a result of modern culture is consequently serious enough. However, in order to avoid one-sidedness and to judge fairly the century in which we live, we must also pay attention to other equally important factors. In the first place, there is the significant phenomenon that culture, as it developed, became more and more unsatisfactory. For a long time, it was thought that [culture] would give man all he needed and would make religion [56] unnecessary for him. But that time is over; the "period of Renan" is already far behind us. There are many reasons for this.

Around the middle of the previous century, culture, or rather the misuse of it and of natural science in particular, led many people toward a crude materialism, in which the soul of man could not live, and which began to pose a serious danger to the highest and noblest goods of humanity. In addition, the more science continued its research, the less it proved able to meet the exaggerated and foolish expectations which had been placed upon it during the first cultural upheaval. As science progressed, the riddles did not diminish but increased; everywhere it saw itself surrounded and limited by mystery; the origin, nature, and end of things remained for it shrouded in an impenetrable darkness. And finally, it became increasingly clear that culture continued to be aristocratic: only a few benefit from [culture] and enjoy its blessings, while the masses are deprived of their privileges. Indeed, it seemed as if science and technology gave capitalism the means to continually strengthen itself and to reduce the poorer classes to the condition of a pitiful proletariat. Slowly but surely, toward the end of the last century, all this brought about a remarkable change.

Science grew in modesty. It became aware of its limitations and once again made room for philosophy which, first following in the footsteps of Kant and then Hegel, sought to build up an idealistic world- and life-view on the basis of the results obtained by the newer sciences. Art, which cannot draw breath in the air of materialism, regained the awareness of [57] its independence and peculiarity. Behind the phenomenon, it went back to the great and mysterious life, and turned away from naturalism and toward symbolism.

Religion, too, was initially restored to its former glory. When modern man returned from nature to himself, he became conscious of the mystery of his own spiritual life; religion appeared to him not to be a vanishing illusion, but an ineradicable ingredient of human nature, and the history of religions bore its seal. Accordingly, in many circles there was an awakening of the religious consciousness, a need for religion. This need was satisfied in the most diverse directions, in Mohammedanism, Buddhism, and *Wotanism*; in art, nature, and human worship; in spiritualism, astrology, and magic. Even socialism, which has attracted the masses because it replaced religion with the promise of a heaven on earth, has lately found many of its advocates to have a more friendly attitude toward religion. Although this revival of religion has not directly benefited Christianity to any great extent, it is in itself of great significance; it proves that man cannot live by bread alone, but only by the word that comes from God's mouth [Matt. 4:4].

Furthermore, it deserves attention that Christianity is not dead but alive. In the circles that have broken away from Christianity this is often misrepresented. Because they have declared it dead themselves, they imagine that it will soon be buried with or without honor. But the reality is quite different. Toward the end of the Middle Ages, many spoke of "the three imposters," but the new era began with the revival of Christian faith both inside and outside the Church of Rome.[1] In the eighteenth century, [58] Rationalism considered itself assured of its victory; and if Christianity had ever been in a weak position it was at that time, for supernaturalism had no power of resistance. And then, under the shock of world events, that mighty movement of revival arose, which gave new life to both Catholicism and Protestantism. Rome has not only risen from its fall but has also regained a prestige and power that hardly anyone thought it capable of and to which culture has surrendered already more than once. In the churches outside of Rome, a different spirit has prevailed, leading to a new life and vigorous action. Above all, one should not forget that Christianity, though quietly, continues from day to day to exert a powerful influence in the hearts of men.

In the Scriptures of the Old and New Testaments, of course, not everything is of equal prominence, nor is everything intended for the same purpose; but in the Psalms and Prophets, in the Gospels and Epistles, there are passages that possess an indestructible vitality and will never fail to move the depths of the soul. In spite of all criticism, the word of God comes to us in Scripture, pulsating with spirit and life. In turn, it reveals itself when it comes to people, whether through reading and examining the Scriptures, in preaching and speaking, or in exhortation or consolation. It can and often does stir up enmity in the human heart; but it can, like no other word, also do good and bless. It evokes the deepest emotions and stirs the soul to its very foundations; it exposes sin, sharpens the sense of guilt, arouses repentance and remorse to the point of shattering the heart, but then it also pours out the consciousness of forgiveness, fills it with joy and gladness, and enables it to live and work anew. [59] And these religious and moral experiences are so powerful and rich that they always triumph over rational reasoning and lead to the confession that in the words of the prophets and apostles God comes to us in a very special way and opens up his fellowship to us. This blessing has always been spread by Christianity, even when its official representatives misused it as *the war machine* (*machine de guerre*) in the struggle against heresy, science, and culture. And from that new life which Christianity manages to inject, there always emerges that powerful action which manifests itself in the most beautiful way in mercy, evangelism, and mission.

This century is also proof of this, and more and more eyes are opened to these important works of Christian love. In particular, the opinion of the mission has changed significantly in recent years. Those who used to despise it and had only a word of pity or ridicule for it are now beginning to praise and support it. Besides, times have changed: the East has awakened and threatens us with a serious danger. Our culture not only shows such dark shades that many flee from it and seek refuge in a return to nature, but we are not even sure we will be able to preserve it and pass it on to our descendants, enriched and amplified.

If (or when) Islam (or Mohammedanism) and Buddhism strengthen themselves and take part in mission, like they do, they will threaten not only Christianity but the whole of our modern culture with decay and ruin.[2] Therefore, the mission is an urgent requirement of our time; it deserves the support of all those who still want to call themselves Christians and who recognize in Christianity an eternal value, of all those who appreciate the noblest goods which God in his providence has given to mankind within Christianity. [60] At present, however, it is still small in power and influence. The few millions of converts won in the last century do not outweigh the enormous losses suffered by Christianity within its own borders, and they are hardly mentioned in comparison with the stupendous growth in which the non-Christian nations may already and increasingly rejoice. Nevertheless, that mission is powerful proof of the vitality of Christianity and one of the most effective weapons in the struggle that Christianity has to wage with its culture, inwardly and outwardly.

As things stand, it is not unfounded to hope that a reconciliation of Christianity and culture, however hostile they may be at present, will be possible. If God has truly come to us in Christ, and if he is also the sustainer and ruler of all things in this age, reconciliation is not only possible but also necessary and will certainly come to light in due course. Some phenomena already seem to point in that direction. It is remarkable that, unlike the rationalism of the "Enlightenment" (*Aufklärung*), the newer philosophy led by Kant and [Johann] Fichte, [Friedrich] Schelling and Hegel, once again sought connection with historic Christianity and at least tried to understand and value it according to its own conception. After the errors of materialism, this philosophy returned and once again led minds in the direction of idealism—that is, of the superiority of spirit over matter. This is still a long way from being Christianity, but it can still pave the way for it.

Furthermore, through research into the lives of the most important naturalists and historians, it has come to light that in their intimate thoughts they had been much closer to Christianity than their followers would have us believe; from their lips often flowed words of appreciation for religion and the [61] Christian religion. Furthermore, the number of those who try to come to terms with Christianity increases almost daily. It is like so: churches, confessions, and dogma often have to pay the price. In our individualistic century every thinker, and even more so everyone who believes himself to be such, considers himself obliged to an independent construction of Christianity, as if the originality of the human spirit

knew no bounds, and every divergent opinion had never been expressed and refuted in previous centuries. Even a foolish idea is
able to find an echo and approval in a like-minded circle.

But all in all, it provides proof that one cannot pass over Christianity indifferently and that the question "What do you think of
the Christ?" remains on the order of the day. In doing so, one
avoids the disappointing expectation that there will ever be a synthesis that satisfies everyone. The unity of the church and Christianity is irrevocably behind us; differentiation is increasing in all
areas, including religion. Just as Roman Catholics and Protestants,
Lutherans and Reformed have had to get used to existing side by
side. God seems to want to teach us even more in this direction; his
teaching in previous centuries of the lack of charity of our hearts
has not yet been received seriously enough.

In the heat of the battle, it is also difficult to acknowledge the
existence and right of existence of other movements; but once the
battle has been fought and the gun smoke has cleared, hostility
often gives way to resignation to the situation and sometimes even
to friendly relations and joint action. Politics provides many examples of this, and the history of Christianity is equally rich with
them. For what gathers and unites all who have been brought up
in Christianity, and in a certain sense even [62] all who bear the
name of man, are the eternal needs of the human heart. Humanity
may progress along its course, but man always remains the same,
his nature appears to be the same everywhere, and his heart can
only be satisfied by God.

After all, his deepest needs always boil down to the fact that
all that is finite rests in the Infinite and Eternal One, who cannot
be thought of in any other way than as a just and holy God who
hates sin and is far removed from wickedness. But if there is to be
any talk of comfort and peace for mankind, then this just and holy
God must also be a merciful and gracious Father, who reconciles
and forgives sin, frees us from guilt, and accepts us as his children

out of grace. And finally, he must also be the Almighty and Faithful One who can realize what he promises and who, in the course of regeneration and sanctification, transforms the world and mankind into a kingdom of God.

These are the ineradicable needs of the human heart. But they are also the basic ideas of Christianity, which stand before us in historical facts as monuments. The apostolic benediction of the love of the Father, the grace of the Son, and of the fellowship of the Holy Spirit is the core of the universal, undoubted, Christian faith [2 Cor. 13:14].

The Christian Faith
Het Christelijke Geloof
(1883)

The Christian Faith (1883)
by Herman Bavinck

[86] It must be acknowledged, although it does not do so to our credit, that the church of today does not measure up in depth and power of confession to those of previous centuries. On the other hand, Christianity in its expansion to all corners is better known than it was in the past. The social and, I would almost say, cosmic power of our Christian faith is better understood than in previous centuries. No one will deny that this aspect of Christian truth must also come into its own. After all, we, along with all the saints, must strive to know not only the depth and the height but also the length and the breadth of Christ's love. But it must not be overlooked that this understanding of the truth is threatened in many people by a serious danger.

It is not by chance that precisely in this [nineteenth] century, attention is drawn to the "breadth and length" of the Christian faith. It relates to the whole character of our time. There is currently a hunger for success, a striving for what is substantial, [for what] has magnitude. The light, the easy attracts. Utilitarianism, the calculation of probabilities, has taken root in our generation and permeates marrow and bone.

The main question is not what is permitted but what is possible, not what is good but what is useful. Harnessing and exploiting everything, so that the greatest possible production is obtained with the least possible effort, is just about everyone's goal and idea. It is not necessary to clarify this with examples; they are there for the taking. In art, especially architecture, the question is what strikes and impresses the superficial observer? *Light* and *compact* are the watchwords. It does not matter what is *in* it, as long as there is something to show *for* it. In schools, both higher and lower, the main issue is how to fill the brain with a wide variety of things in the shortest possible time. And trade and [87] industry are driven by calculation, not by what is provided but by what is obtained. Speculation is the soul of it.

The same lack of depth can also be seen in the domain of the higher life. In religion and morality, one tries as quickly as possible to acquire a *modus vivendi*, a way of life with which one can make do without being called uncivilized and improper. God, virtue, immortality, together with a few easy rules for morality, and the religious-moral person of our time, in his opinion, is already even this hour suitable for heaven. To delve deeper is a waste of time, and time is money. Serious self-examination is unnecessary; it is detrimental to the affair, and it can only be tolerated to a certain extent in foolish types. The interests of the soul must not be given too much thought. What could [the soul] want? Later when things are going well, the individual will be satisfied, and it will say, "Behold, you have laid up many goods for many years."

The superficial sense—that disregard for quality and content, that reckoning with the masses—can also be observed among confessors of Jesus Christ. There is a confession, yes, but without glow; often driven by excitement and by party enthusiasm; seldom by the urge of the heart and deep inner experience. We confess, but as if in secret and almost with a feeling of shame. We often distrust the grounds of our faith and shy away from examination. It is as if we are in peril. Undoubtedly, in the past we were called to profess our most holy faith, but who today still boldly repeats it? There is enough party enthusiasm and party interest, but faith, inspiration, vivacity, admiration, holy verve—where do we find them today? We have forgotten how to confess.[1]

The reason for this is not hard to find. The world has dominated us with its imagination and representations and has encroached upon the life of the church. We imagine far too often that the society in which we live still allows itself to be shaped and governed by the confession of the church, just as it was in the previous three centuries. This is not the case. I do not want to deny that there are traces and aftereffects of it here and there. But the source from which the nations now derive their moral, civil, political principles, and ideas has become an entirely different one. Society has changed. It has emancipated itself from Christianity and the Reformation. Innocent and suspecting no wrongdoing, the community has allowed itself to be influenced by this revolution more than it knows. It has adopted concepts, thoughts, and imaginations without criticism. Principles and methods of research, results, and even a large part of the dictionary of the revolution have been accepted by [the community] without thought. That [88] makes us powerless. It makes us mistrust our own faith and its foundations. On the other hand, we must again come to realize that the church of Christ has a completely different life than the world. We must take seriously the truth that whoever believes in Jesus Christ is truly a different, a new person. Only in faith should we seek our strength and power and therefore abandon all attempts to make a compromise between the church and the world. Both are diametrically opposed to each other. It is a life-and-death struggle. Therefore, it should not surprise us at all if the world considers our faith to be foolishness and rejects it as an absurdity. That is only natural. It is rather surprising that they still retain so much of our faith. That only happens by grace, by disloyalty to its own principle, as a weak but ever weakening aftereffect of a glorious past.

Let me make these statements clear by briefly pointing out the *character*, *foundation*, and *content* of our faith.

The life of the church is a life of faith. [The church] lives out of, through, and in faith. All its actions, thoughts, words, knowledge, and deeds are in this domain. What does this mean? Simply that the church, living out of the unseen, professes to be the exact opposite of what the author of the book of material things teaches. The outward appearance of things, the appearance of things, is against it. This reveals itself in the smallest and most minor of things. "Creation does not preach a loving God," so they say, but the church confesses and proudly holds up against all objections: "God is love." They say, "There is no other world but this one; this one is the best; there is no better one." And the church replies, "There is another and better one; a kingdom of unseen and eternal goods that is sure to come; this world is a fallen one and leads to nowhere." They go on to say that the Bible is so strange and a source of so much irritation, and the church confesses, "The Bible is God's Word." They say, "The crucified one is an annoyance and a foolishness to us." But to us, the church confesses, "He is the power of God and the wisdom of God; the crucified one is my Lord and my God, my only glory and my life's strength." "My conscience accuses me," says the church, "of having sinned grievously against all God's commandments and still being inclined to all evil; and yet," she continues, "I am righteous before God." From that day that the fathers fell asleep, all things remain the same from the beginning of the creation, and yet we expect a new heaven and a new earth. That is the *nevertheless* of faith. Poor and nevertheless rich; having nothing and nevertheless possessing everything; guilty of death and damnation and nevertheless an heir [89] of eternal life; a citizen of hell, and nevertheless a citizen of heaven. Faith places this "nevertheless" between two sets of tremendous opposites. One set teaches: this is how it appears; against which, the other declares: but this is how it is. This is how it appears, according to the standard of this fallen and transient world; this is how it is, according to the rule of the other and better world, which is the real world, and to which it must lead, and into which it must once pass. By all appearances, according to what these visible things teach you, you are right, O world: there is no God, no heaven, no holiness, and no glory. Whatever befalls the children of men befalls the beasts also, and some befalls them both. He who sees the breath of man ascending, and the breath of beast descending, into the earth. But in opposition to this doctrine of the visible, faith recognizes that the things one does not see are so wonderful, so powerful, and [it] places in contrast to the knowledge of *appearances* the knowledge of *faith*. Our faith is one great, awesome paradox, a miracle from beginning to end. Faith is simply putting God in the right; everything else, mankind and the world together, [is] in the wrong. It tears off the blindfold of delusion, awakening [one] from a long oppressive dream—coming to one's senses, coming to oneself out of an intoxicating stupor. It is an acknowledgement. Things, including myself, are not as I see them with my clouded view and my short-sighted vision, but are as God sees them from the depths of his glory. Therefore, on the one hand, it is a denial of ourselves, of our mind and will, of our feelings and imagination, of all things, of the entire world. But on the other hand, it is a reliance on God, a humble confession: "Thou, O my God, art right; thy word is truth." In order to live up to this statement of faith with a joyful conscience, one needs a moral strength that is given only to a few. Not just anyone is able to do that. No study or research can ever get us that far. To put forth a completely different order of things against all appearances, against all the pronouncements of science; to see folly in the wisdom of the world and to honor the highest wisdom in the folly of the cross' to go against ourselves and to accept the very opposite of what we have wanted, felt, thought, believed—that is, a moral, spiritual demonstration of strength, which is impossible for any human being after the fall into sin and only becomes possible through the powerful working of the Holy Spirit. Believing in the truth of the unseen is only possible through the power of the unseen himself. To see the kingdom of heaven, one [90] must stand in it and, through regeneration, become a citizen of it.

Therefore, the world cannot believe. It lacks the moral fortitude to perform such a heroic deed; it is too weak and unspiritual for it; if she could, she would cease to be the world. If for a time, [the world] was under the influence of the power of faith and the heroic confession of the church of Christ, it was held back in restraint and did not manifest its true nature; it was in spite of itself; and the first opportunity it saw, it shook off the yoke of the church and emancipated itself. Outside the church, there is no real faith, no soul-binding conviction of the reality of the invisible. Then there is only opinion, perspective, insight, guess, conjecture. Outside of faith, there is no firmness of conviction, and therefore one must always say, "In my opinion," "according to me it seems," "as it seems to me," "in my mind,"—phrases of which we have no lack of in this time. Thus always, it seems to me "there is a God," "there is virtue," "there is immortality," "there is heaven or hell," "Jesus is the Christ." An existence of all the invisible by the grace of man's pleasure. A proclamation of the existence of the Godhead by senatorial edict, by the majority, by the half plus one.[2]

Independent of all human judgment, resolutely and boldly confessing "there is a God and by his grace I am what I am" is something the church can profess alone, but the world cannot profess. Nevertheless, it is true that sometimes the world also expresses its denials in a bold and insolent manner. When it begins to tire of individualism, it sees no salvation or escape except in the systematization of its unbelief. Then [the world] becomes doctrinally fanatical and erects funeral pyres for those who believe with their hearts and profess with their mouths. The world is always moving between these two: either indifference, nominalism, anarchy, abandonment of all objective truth in favor of the opinions of the few, denial of all absolutes on the one hand; or absolutism, state absolutism, autocracy, determination of truth by the strongest position on the other. It always hovers between a realism without an ideal, which is absorbed in the deification of matter and fleshly service, and an idealism without reality, which therefore needs the strong arm of the despot to exist.

On the other hand, the church makes its confession without any doubt or hesitation, firmly and powerfully, with the steadfastness of a martyr and the humility of someone praying. It can do both because for it, idea and fact are one; the unseen, the spiritual, the eternal things are for it the highest reality, much more real [91] than what we behold here with our physical eye. That there is a God, that Jesus is the Christ, that there is a kingdom of heaven are even more certain to her than a mathematical axiom. If the opposite were possible, [the church] would sooner doubt the sunlight that falls into its eye than the reality of the higher world that sends its rays into its soul. For [the church] is convinced of the truth of the poet's words, that the earthly is but a likeness of the eternal and God's existence is the cornerstone and foundation of all truths. [The church] knows that the form of this world, the appearance of things, which so enchants us, is passing away; and eternal and imperishable is the unseen, which opens up and makes itself known only to those who believe. Therefore, the church is skeptical, distrustful of anyone who wants to loosen that attachment, or even reverse the order. God must remain God, so that man can remain man. The faith of the church therefore excludes all doubt and is the opposite of individualistic thinking. And yet, strange as it may seem, by that same faith, the church is protected from exercising even the slightest constraints of conscience. After, all, convinced in the soul of the reality of the higher world, [the church] knows and accepts that [the church] does not carry [the higher world], but that this [higher world] carries and maintains [the church]; that it therefore lives only from and through [the higher world], and cannot add to or subtract from its real existence. In faith, [the church] does not hurry. The spiritual world maintains itself; the church, living out of it, has only to testify of it and never has to do anything else other than to proclaim loudly, powerfully, confidently, full of the Holy Spirit, before all the world: "I believe."

If we accept that faith excludes all doubt, then what is the ground on which it rests, what is the proof that this faith is also not a dream or an illusion? It is the peculiarity of the Christian faith that it cannot be deduced or explained from any of the forces present in nature and man. It is not the fruit of reason, nor the result of intellectual argumentation or scientific research; it has nothing to do with a syllogistic decision. Nor is it the result of any effort of the will, as if [the will] were capable of attaining such by itself; for the fact is, wanting to believe like this is impossible. Nor is it the fruit of the senses or the product of the imagination, for it is essentially different in nature from both and is prior to them both. It cannot be explained by man or by the authorities of this fallen world. We saw clearly that it consisted precisely in the complete negation of everything that belongs to this visible world, of ourselves in the first place, of all of our thoughts and ideas and inclinations. The belief of the unbeliever is the [92] complete opposite of this. It is, in the words of the apostle, a substitution of God's truth for a lie, an honoring of the creature for the Creator, a failure to appreciate the unseen in order to seek refuge in the visible. Whatever form this belief takes, it always rests on something that belongs to this world; it is based on a force within man, on his intellectual reasoning or his rich imagination. It continues to move in a circle and never leaves that circle of enchantments. It is always idolatry, never religion, because it does not rest on a word from God but on a notion of mankind. The true, genuine Christian faith, however, is a complete renunciation of all things, a crucifixion and burial of oneself, a spiritual experience in which everything we previously trusted in disappears. Therefore, if [faith] does not rest in anything of mankind, but on the contrary gives up and forsakes everything and then rises again from that death of self-crucifixion, yes it brings us another, new, holy life which we did not know before; then after all, it can only rest in the living God. The life of faith that is born of total self-denial, of death, cannot have its origin except in him who brought life out of death into immortality. Faith, which makes us grasp the unseen things and, in a word, makes us live out of them and at the same time, is a revelation of power from the higher world itself, which cannot be explained from this world. Faith in Christ is therefore a gift, a powerful revelation of the Spirit. On account of faith's supernatural origin, it brings with it not only its own certainty, but also the reality of its object of the invisible things. Without this, [faith] could not exist. Therefore, faith is a guarantee for things hoped for and an assurance of things unseen [Heb. 11:1]. What the poet sang to the discoverer of the New World, that if it did not exist it would have to rise out of the sea, is in fact true of Christian faith. The gift of the Spirit is, for him who has it, the final proof of the Spirit's existence and of all that he communicates.

How this faith is worked in our hearts cannot be fully described. The working of the Spirit is so wonderful, so unfathomable, and nearly impossible to put into words. We are confronted here with a miracle and with a mystery. This I know: it is not attained by historical-critical research and theoretical studies. Nor by a favorable predisposition or a solid character. It is worked into us by a powerful, immediate impression, at the very moment when the reality [93] of spiritual things powerfully and irresistibly thrusts itself upon our souls and proclaims itself as truth. Suddenly, a light then dawns on us that shows us the misery of "below" and the holiness and glory of "above."

We have a weak analogy with this indescribable impression in the way in which the moral law powerfully announces itself as a real power in the conscience of every human being. There is also an analogy in the strange phenomenon that the most wonderful thoughts suddenly fall into our consciousness and are perceived as a gift. Thus with Athanasius, the firm conviction of the divinity of the Son and with Augustine, the certainty of election was awakened by an immediate impression (*onmiddellijken indruk*); and with Luther, justification by faith alone was unshakably established. No article of our confession rests on intellectual research or scientific investigation; these always came after. What gave a dogma subjective assurance and its confessors strength and courage of conviction was always that immediate (*onmiddellijken*), indescribable impression (*onbeschrijflijke indruk*) of its truth in the heart through the Spirit. Only then is our faith true when it becomes impossible for us to believe otherwise: that "I cannot do other than; I must not do other than," that gives our faith the power to overcome the world, that makes every article of our faith the product of a deep spiritual experience, a spiritual gain, by reverently accepting, if we ourselves may find the truth of it so powerfully expressed in our hearts.

However, this impression (*onmiddellijk*) is not created in us so immediately that the Holy Spirit would exclude any possible means. As in the natural world, conviction in the spiritual realm is also "mediated" (*vermittelt*) by the Word. Only the Word can awaken this conviction in us. The Holy Spirit must be spoken into our hearts by the Holy Spirit, in such a tone and with such emphasis as he alone, who brought forth the Word, is able to do and then it leaves an indelible impression (*onuitwischbaren indruk*) in our souls. Then the truth of it is unquestionably sealed in our hearts. This faith, then, is something so tender and holy that it can rest only in God—in no one else, in no book or writing—only and exclusively in God. But then still in God, who speaks to me in his written word and confirms the truth of it to my heart by his Holy Spirit. God, his word, his promises, his deeds are the pillars on which my faith rests. It is facts, deeds, and history that form its foundation, and whose inseparable connection with the truth sealed in us guarantees its future. Therefore, if you will, we believe [95] in authority, in the authority of God himself, who works in us by his Spirit a joyful faith in him and his word. And so little is that authority a compulsion or force, that faith itself knows no greater joy than to rest in that authority of God. Yes, it would die and wither if it rested in anything else but God. For it is firm and certain, not because it is faith but because its faith is in God; it is strong and the conqueror of the world, because its faith in Christ overcomes the world; it is holy and glorious, because its faith is in the Holy Spirit.

Standing in that faith, living through [that faith], the church also expresses what it believes. [The church] neither hides nor is ashamed of its confession. Assured and full of confidence, [the church] speaks it joyfully, even though the funeral pyres are smoking. Yes, in the glow of martyrdom, its confession was often the most powerful; what was experienced in the soul automatically forced itself upon its lips. [The church] confessed and could not confess otherwise. That is the impulse of its heart; [the church] cannot remain silent; its believes and therefore it speaks. [The church] must testify of God's miracles, mention his majestic deeds. Is the Holy Scripture not enough for it? Oh, most certainly, this is its only source; from [the Scripture] everything flows to [the church], in its depths [the church] dives again and again. Scripture is the magnificent painting which, in a series of captivating scenes, brings before our eyes the works of God in salvation history. Well then, that powerful imprint which the Scriptures make on [the church], it must reproduce. What [the church] has seen through that wonderful book, what it has felt of the word of life, it must proclaim. [The church] must try to put it into words and account for it. [The church] has absorbed what the Scriptures tell it, lived it as it were, and now reproduces it in its confession. Emerging again from the penetration of the Holy Scriptures, it looks around itself, feels strange in this world, and expresses to opponents and those who are astray—with holy enthusiasm—what it has experienced and enjoyed. [The church] does not create; it does not discover a single truth; it only finds what is laid down in Scripture; it merely reflects *after* the Holy Spirit has *thought* it all out, but then [the church] expresses what it has found and thus reflects in its own language, in its own way, fully conscious, and understandable for everyone. The confession it expresses, therefore, does not stand above or beside or outside Scripture, but entirely *in* Scripture. From this [the church] is wrought, through the channel of congregational experience.

Naturally, that did not happen all at once; what is contained in that Bible is so rich and so broad in scope that it cannot be taken in and reproduced by one person, not [95] by a single generation of people. That requires centuries. The knowledge of the length and breadth and depth and height of Christ's love can only be attained in fellowship with *all* the saints. First, therefore, the confession is small. Nothing else is needed except: I believe in Jesus, the Christ. Later on, it will be explained more broadly in the words: I believe in the Father, the Son, and the Holy Spirit. That is the root, which later on grows into the trunk of the twelve articles of faith. And each time the church is introduced more deeply into God's revelation in subsequent times, this root grows up and various branches grow on it, some of which bend sideways and grow in the wrong direction. But thus, in the course of the centuries, the love of Christ is interpreted more and more broadly, and that glorious image which the church conceives from the Holy Scriptures and causes to radiate outwardly is further and further completed.

It is hard to say what [the church] is already professing because it is so rich and so deep. [The church] believes in God. It thinks about him, it meditates upon him, it testifies about him. Of God always, of God alone. Of the deeds that he has wrought from ancient times, which he continues to work until the end of the centuries. [The church] lives from God, it rests in him, it speaks of him, of his being and attributes, of his works and wonders, of him in the entire riches of his self-revelation, in the unsearchable fullness of his beings, in the Trinity of his existence. In his works, it sees three circles, in his existence three ways, never separated, always distinguished, reflecting itself also in its own spiritual experience. The inexhaustible riches of the divine life and being manifest itself in his self-revelation, which is expressed and represented by the church in its confession of the trinitarian God. First of all, the church, beautifully distinguished from the world, feels absolutely dependent on an absolute power, which called [the church] and all things out and still maintains and rules over them. For [the church], however, this power is not an impersonal fate, not a subdued thought, but a divine independence who knows and wants, rules and directs it, which [the church] addresses as "Thou" and to whom it voluntarily and unconditionally bows. [The church] confesses him as the Creator of heaven and earth, who in the divine being exists as one in himself, from whom all things derive their origin, the sovereign, the lawgiver, the judge of all things. Nonetheless, it also confesses him as the Father, Father of the Son, and through [the Son], Father also of his children on earth, whom he cares for and guards as the apple of his eye. Gleaning all this from the Holy Scriptures and experiencing it themselves in their souls, the congregation raises its eyes to heaven in thanksgiving and confesses: *I believe in God,* [96] *the Father Almighty, Creator of Heaven and Earth.*

But [the church] confesses even more. Yes, if it had no more to confess, it would be unable to confess even this little with reason alone. The world honors neither the Creator nor the Father except in name alone. But the church believes in the Father because it also believes in the Son. And here, the church is now at the heart of its confession. Jesus Christ is the center of all its knowledge and faith. [The church] wants nothing but to know of him, the crucified one. Think of him, consider him, describe him; of his eternal generation from the Father to his conception and birth from Mary; and from there, it follows him throughout his life into his death and burial; and when he rose and ascended to heaven, then [the church] looks after him, keeping an eye above where Christ is, believing that in time he will return upon the clouds of heaven.

Through him, [the church] rejoices; a complete reversal has been brought about. [Christ] has restored the relationship of all things to God, which had been disturbed by sin. He has reconciled all things to God, including mankind. Heaven and earth, God and man, Jew and Gentile, Greek and Barbarian—all are reconciled. He brought about that powerful reversal, not by force of arms but only by suffering. His entire life is summarized by the church in the word: he who suffered. Through the cross alone, he has triumphed over the principalities and powers. That was his only weapon. Alone and never in anything other than in the sign of the cross, he has achieved victory. That is the point: all things are reconciled and reunified. Just as everything turned away from God through the tree of knowledge, so everything returns to God through the cross. After having accomplished reconciliation, he now proceeds to gather all things under him as the head in the fullness of time— everything that is in heaven and on earth [Eph. 1:10]. As king he will reign until all his enemies are laid under his feet. Considering all this now, the church once again raises its eye with vivacity and declares, *I believe in Jesus Christ, his only begotten Son, our Lord.*

But even more is included in this confession of faith. The reconciliation is there. But then the questions arise: How am I going to stand in it, how do I participate in it, when the unholy powers of sin inside and outside of me carry me farther and farther from Christ? What is the divine power that disengages me from my unholy self and brings me into fellowship with Christ? What power drives us to Christ [97] and to his cross? The church has the answer ready. There is another one: a guide in truth, a comforter who, proceeding from God, returns to Christ and thus returns to the Father, who is not of this world though [he] works in it, and who rebirths and renews us. And the church, looking up the third time, confesses: *I believe in the Holy Spirit.*

Threefold is he, the true living God whom the church worships. He is threefold in existence, one in essence. For if [the church] did not know that the Father was God, it could not rely on him. If it did not know that the Son was God, it could not rest on his satisfaction for time and eternity. If [the church] did not know that the Holy Spirit was God, it could not rely on his testimony and could not entrust herself to his guidance. [If we] take away just one of these three ways, [then] salvation will falter in our souls and the assurance of faith is impossible. But since God is above, before, and in us, and we are surrounded, cared for, preserved by God on all sides, we may even now have rest and peace, for salvation is certain. If God is for us, then who will be against us [Rom. 8:31]? From him and through him and unto him are all things; to him be the glory [Rom. 11:36].

But who will honor him? Once more the church raises its voice and declares, *I believe in one holy catholic Christian church.* [The church] is there and it will be completed despite the attacks and the gates of hell. Through the forgiveness of sins and the resurrection of the flesh, [the church] will certainly be restored to eternal life. There is no doubt about it. This is where all the works of the three divine persons are directed. One in essence, they are also one in purpose. [The church] is the temple they build together and desire for dwelling. And when the elements burn and the earth and its works perish, then this temple, which God has labored for centuries, will arise gloriously upon the ruins of sin and abide forever.

Afterword

The past decade has seen a remarkable renaissance of interest in the work of Herman Bavinck, the great Dutch theologian, whose life spanned the last decades of the nineteenth century and the early decades of the twentieth century. Bavinck's contribution as a public theologian has mostly resided in the shadows of his more famous contemporary, Abraham Kuyper. The recently renewed interest in Bavinck comes as a reminder that Bavinck loomed large in the minds not only of the Dutch people but as a significant public voice on both sides of the Atlantic. A century removed, it is difficult to fathom that professional theologians such as Bavinck were figures of immense importance in the public arena of modern Western culture. Unlike most contemporary theologians in our own day, Bavinck was not relegated to the backwaters of academia. As James Eglinton has reminded, Bavinck was virtually a household name throughout the Netherlands.

It is therefore noteworthy that Greg Parker has brought out the first English translation of Bavinck's work describing (and defending) Christianity to an increasingly religiously pluralistic European culture. In a series of short expositions of the major religions of the world, this little work will prove a much more accessible work than Bavinck's many more theologically dense writings. It also provides a window into the way public religious discourse carried on at the end of the nineteenth century in the context of increasing religious pluralism. It also lends a unique angle of perspective into Bavinck's own relationship to the increasing theological liberalism of his day. He was resolutely orthodox in his theological commitments, as this work makes apparent, while his tone throughout is resolutely chari-table toward those with whom he has disagreements.

At the outset of the work, Bavinck indicates how difficult his assignment is: to describe Christianity in a cultural context where there are significant differences between different kinds of Chris-tians. And from the beginning, Bavinck makes it clear that these matters should not be treated as if nothing hinges on the outcome. Christianity matters because Christ matters, and Christ matters because eternity hangs in the balance. This is no mere neutral de-piction of the Christian religion.

The history of Christianity serves as the fundamental lens for Bavinck throughout. In retrospect, there are two important points to highlight. The beginning of Christian history does not start with the early church, but inside the Christian Scriptures themselves. In particular, Bavinck's opening concern highlights the historical na-ture of the Gospel narratives of Jesus and why it matters if one is to understand Christianity at all. In this, Bavinck provides a thought-ful and concise defense of the claim that the Jesus of the Gospels is the Jesus of history, and that the Jesus of history is also the Lord of the universe. The second point to be drawn at the outset is Bavinck's resolute willingness to disagree with the growing major-ity of critical scholars in his own day regarding the reliability of the Gospel accounts. Bavinck's defense of Jesus focuses not on histori-cal documentation but on the basis of the theological claims laid out clearly in the ministry of Jesus. So, for example, Bavinck spends considerable time with the claim that Jesus makes not merely as a prophet of the kingdom but as the king himself, though surely an unusual king. He does not merely honor the Sabbath but is the Lord of the Sabbath. These sorts of claims are hard to square with the modern notion that Jesus is a good teacher but nothing more.

Aside from the usefulness of this work for Bavinck specialists, it also should prove valuable for contemporary Christians as they interact with a world even more deeply religiously pluralistic than

Bavinck's world. At first glance in this work, Bavinck appears more of a religious historian, but a careful read will highlight the manner in which he graciously describes disagreements in church history that remained significant in his own time (and in ours as well). He carefully and sympathetically depicts the opposing sides, and then carefully analyzes the internal consistency as well as the reasons why on its own terms the position is not emotionally or intellectually satisfying. The section on Roman Catholicism is especially to be commended in this regard. For a conservative Protestant still living in the shadow of deep animosity between Rome and Protestants, Bavinck ably depicts Catholic dogma carefully, graciously, and fairly. In the end, he clearly distinguishes himself from Rome but does so with a careful historian's eye to detail.

Of particular interest to contemporary Reformed Protestants is Bavinck's description of the three streams of the Protestant Reformation: Luther, Calvin, and Zwingli. Bavinck sees the central differences between these magisterial Reformers having to do with their diverse understandings of the law. Luther interpreted the gospel as a response to a sinner's failure to live in accordance with the law. By contrast, Zwingli saw the gospel as freedom from the law, leaving the Christian no longer a bondservant of the law.

For Calvin, the law was but one issue addressed by the gospel. As Bavinck writes, "For Calvin, the law was not seen in the one-sided light in which Luther saw it, and consequently, although justification was a very important benefit, it was not the only benefit of the gospel" [page 45]. For Calvin, the consequences of the gospel extend across the whole breadth of human endeavors, from social and political matters, to education, psychology, and family matters. The gospel transforms the way in which all of these spheres of human interactions carry on. In this regard, according to Bavinck, it was Calvin who saw the full breadth of the impact of the gospel and thereby the one who most fully brought the Reformation into the modern world.

At the dawn of the modern era, the medieval unity of church and culture effectively broke down. With the demise of ecclesiastical and social unity came a new kind of religious and national pluralism. Actual church attendance remained well below 50 percent of the population in most of Europe, even while the historical memory of Christianity as the "official religion" remained strong. By the eighteenth century, the recognition of alternative accounts of Christianity, as well as alternative religious systems present throughout Europe, offered a new public consciousness.

As Peter Berger argued at the end of the twentieth century, a plethora of alternative religious options undermines the certainty associated with religiously homogenous cultures. People are prone to doubt the validity of any singular religious claim since there are so many diverse competitors. Berger referred to this as the "heretical imperative." The seeds of this new form of doubt entered the public realm in Bavinck's time, and he took them quite seriously. Was historic Christianity viable in the modern world of so many religious options?

Bavinck's own father, a conservative minister in the Seceder church in the Netherlands, did not want his son to be educated at the "modern" university at Leiden for fear that his mind would be corrupted by so many diverse viewpoints. The younger Bavinck remained loyal to the historic orthodoxy of his father, but he realized the doubts raised by the modern world had to be addressed carefully and thoughtfully. As the younger Bavinck came to understand his cultural milieu, the gravest doubts he encountered centered around the supernatural elements of Christianity. Bavinck clearly saw that doubts about the supernatural would undermine the very essence of Christianity and result in a flattening of human identity, whose only telos would become its own temporal survival.

From a very different angle, the great German atheist Friedrich Nietzsche effectively agreed with Bavinck's diagnosis, arguing that the only values left in a world without God would be health and happiness, neither of which could ever be ultimately satisfied. According to Bavinck, doubts about supernatural elements led inevitably to a shrinking of the human heart in such a fashion that only concerns about the transitory world would matter—what Charles Taylor would later refer to as the "immanent frame." Bavinck well understood what was at stake in the defense of Christian supernaturalism.

Surprisingly, the twentieth century saw a revival of religion; but not surprising, it was too often rooted in the unsatisfying nature of a worldview without transcendence or meaning. As Bavinck tells the story, carried alongside of the revival of a generic or civil religion was also a renewal of genuine Christian faith. This was evidence to Bavinck that the word of God breaks through even the most hardened of secular worldviews, both because it is true and alone is satisfying to the human heart. Bavinck's confidence rested finally in the power of the Holy Spirit to accomplish what God himself promised. The human heart can only be satisfied by the Living God, and though attempts will continue to avoid God, his truth and justice will prevail.

The concerns Bavinck raises in this little work are not dissimilar to those we now face in the early decades of the twenty-first century. There are many religious options in our age, including the option of decrying all religious options, and the rise of the secular spirit runs strong in many contexts. The question facing Christians is how shall we respond? It is Bavinck's model of careful historical analysis, keen theological insight, and especially the courage and compassion of his work that deserve to be emulated. It is with this conviction that it is hoped Bavinck's treatise will receive a wide and varied readership in the English-speaking world and leave its wise imprint on its readers for many years to come.

Richard Lints
Consulting Theologian
Redeemer City to City Ministry
New York City

Notes

Translator's Preface

1. Herman Bavinck, *Reformed Dogmatics*, vols. I–IV, trans. John Vriends and ed. John Bolt (Grand Rapids: Baker Academic, 2003–8); Bavinck, *Gereformeerde Dogmatiek*, Deel I–IV, 2e druk (Kampen: J. H. Kok, 1906–11).

2. Herman Bavinck, "Het Christendom," Groote Godsdiensten ser. II, no. 7 (Baarn: Hollandia-Drukkerij, 1912).

3. See also Bavinck, "Het Wezen des Christendoms," in *Almanak van het studentencorps a/d Vrije Universiteit*, ed. J. F. van Beeck Calkoen, J. H. Broeks Roelofs, H. C. Rutgers, A.A. van Schelven, and J. Thijs (Amsterdam: Herdes, 1906), 251–77; Bavinck, "The Essence of Christianity," in *Essays on Religion, Science, and Society*, ed. John Bolt, trans. Harry Boonstra and Gerrit Sheeres (Grand Rapids: Baker Academic, 2008), 33–48; and James Eglinton, *Bavinck: A Critical Biography* (Grand Rapids: Baker Academic, 2020), 276–77.

4. Bavinck, *Guidebook for Instruction in the Christian Religion*, trans. and eds. Gregory Parker Jr. and Cameron Clausing (Peabody, MA: Hendrickson, 2022); Bavinck, *Handleiding bij het Onderwijs in den Christelijken Godsdienst* (Kampen: J. H. Kok, 1913).

5. Eglinton, *Bavinck*, 262. See Bruce Pass, "Introduction," in Bavinck, *On Theology: Herman Bavinck's Academic Orations* (Leiden: Brill, 2020), 1–29.

6. Herman Bavinck, "Het Christelijk Geloof," *De Vrije Kerk* 9:1, 2, 4 (January, February, April 1883): 44–47; 90–95; 184–93. Republished in *Kennis en leven: opstellen en artikelen uit vroegere jaren, verzameld door Ds C. B. Bavinck* (Kampen: J. H. Kok, 1922), 86-97.

7. Rowan Williams, *What Is Christianity?* (New York: Church Publishing, 2016).

8. Bonhoeffer is a prime example of another theologian asking the "Who" question. In his lectures on Christology, he makes a distinction between the "How?" and "Who?" questions. "How?" is the question of the

serpent, the question of fallen Adam. "Who are you?" is the true question one must ask before Christ. See Dietrich Bonhoeffer, *Berlin: 1932–1933*, ed. Carsten Nicolaisen, Ernst-Albert Scharffenorth, and Larry L. Rasmussen, trans. Isabel Best, David Higgins, and Douglas W. Stott, vol. 12, *Dietrich Bonhoeffer Works* (Minneapolis, MN: Fortress Press, 2009), 299–360.

9. Eglinton, *Bavinck*, 277.

10. Bavinck, *Reformed Dogmatics*, IV, 107–8.

11. Pass likewise notes that in Bavinck's *Philosophy of Revelation*, Bavinck argues for the existence of God from the phenomenology of religion. See Pass, "Introduction," 19; and Bavinck, *Philosophy of Revelation: A New Annotated Edition*, ed. Cory Brock, and Nathaniel Sutanto (Peabody, MA: Hendrickson, 2018), 66–68.

12. See also Bavinck, *Reformed Dogmatics*, IV, 279–81.

13. See page 20.

14. See Bavinck, *Reformed Dogmatics*, IV, 298–99.

15. Bavinck, *Reformed Dogmatics*, IV, 320–25.

16. See page 46.

17. Nathaniel Sutanto, "Confessional, International, and Cosmopolitan: Herman Bavinck's Neo-Calvinistic and Protestant Vision of the Catholicity of the Church," in *Journal of Reformed Theology* 12, no. 1 (2018): 22–39, 31. Sutanto's judgment of Bavinck's catholic-Calvinisim holds true.

18. Bavinck's description of the various "pressures" that led from the version of Christianity that featured in the Middle Ages to the eighteenth century has continuity with Charles Taylor's assessment of the shifting axioms of faith. See Charles Taylor, *A Secular Age* (Cambridge: Harvard University Press, 2007.

19. See page 54.

20. Williams, *What Is Christianity?*, 1–25.

21. See Bavinck, *Reformed Dogmatics*, IV, 320. Bavinck might make the criticism against Williams's reliance on external practices/forms as providing the unity.

22. Bruce Pass, *The Heart of Dogmatics: Christology and Christocentricism in Herman Bavinck* (Göttingen: Vandenhoeck & Ruprecht, 2020), 83–84. Pass locates development in Bavinck's theology that can be tied to his reflections on the essence of Christianity. In his reflections on the essence of Christianity, Bavinck places Christ as both the "content" and "center" of Christianity. The deity of Christ functions then as the irreducible "minimum" of Christianity. Christ, as Pass notes, functions not only as the center of a system of doctrine but as the "lifeblood" of religion. This casts a helpful hue to Bavinck's attention to lived religion.

23. Williams, *What Is Christianity?*, 3–7.

24. In 1916, this pamphlet was translated by Dr. Rev. Albert A. Pfanstiehl as "Christ and Christianity," in *The Biblical Review* I (1916): 214–36. He was a minister in the Chicago area and a classmate of Henry Dosker at Hope College; see "Authors among Our Alumni," *The Anchor* 36, no. 4 (October 24, 1923), 4. Just prior to completing his translation, Pfanstiehl spent time in the Netherlands as a preacher to interned soldiers; see "Pfanstiehl to Tour United States," in *The Highland Park Press* 43, no. 5 (December 23, 1915), 1. Pfanstiehl's translation is a paraphrase of the original. He also tended to expand or constrict Bavinck's writing, such that the later portions of Pfanstiehl's translation of "Het Christendom" is almost entirely Pfanstiehl.

Chapter 1

1. Bavinck is referring to Immanuel Kant, Georg Hegel, Friedrich Schleiermacher, Albrecht Ritschl, Adolf von Harnack, Rudolf Eucken, Thomas Green, and Edward Caird.

2. This phrase "original Christianity" (*oorspronkelijke Christendom*) appears several times in Bavinck's other essay on the "essence of Christianity." See Bavinck, "Het Wezen des Christendoms," 255, 263–64, 267, 268–69, 270–71; Bavinck, "The Essence of Christianity" (missing from the translation on page 35), 37–40, 42–44, 46. The phrase "original Christianity" is meant to be placed polemically in conversation with Strauss and Harnack. For our sake, Bavinck is simply arguing that Christianity has developed beyond the meager confession of the first Christians, such that it is impossible for the church to go back to some sort of "original" form. See Cameron Clausing, "'A Christian Dogmatic Does Not *Yet* Exist': The Influence of the Nineteenth Century Historical Turn on the Theological Method of Herman Bavinck" (PhD diss., University of Edinburgh, 2020), 75.

3. See also Bavinck, *Handleiding bij het Onderwijs in den Christelijken Godsdienst*, 44.

4. See Adolf van Harnack, *History of Dogma*, vol. III (Edinburgh: William & Norgate, 1897), 184, 197–98, 220–22; and Bavinck, *Reformed Dogmatics* III, 265–74.

5. This is a reference to the "Historical Jesus" movement. Albert Schweitzer's book *The Quest for the Historical Jesus*, translated into English in 1910, largely subdued the movement. See Schweitzer, *The Quest for the Historical Jesus*, trans. W. M Montgomery (London: Adam and Charles Black, 1910); and Schweitzer, *Von Reimarus zu Wrede: eine Geschichte der Leben-Jesu-*

Forschung (Tübingen: Mohr, 1906). "From Paul and John we have to go back to the Jesus of the Synoptics, especially to the Jesus of the Sermon on the Mount." Bavinck provides the full quote in his *Reformed Dogmatics* (see III, 267), in which he attributes this saying to the followers of Albrecht Ritschl.

Chapter 2

1. In Dutch, it's about "de beschikking van zijn Vader" and Jesus' dependence on it.

2. For a superb reading on Bavinck's modified appropriation of Schleiermacher, see Cory Brock, *Orthodox yet Modern: Herman Bavinck's Use of Friedrich Schleiermacher* (Bellingham, WA: Lexham Press, 2020).

3. See Bavinck, *Reformed Dogmatics* III, 386–93.

4. Bavinck draws this idea from Wilhelm Baldensperger's *Das Selbstbewusstsein Jesu im Lichte der messianischen Hoffnungen seiner Zeit* (Strasburg: J. H. E. Heitz and Mündel, 1888), 114. Baldensperger contends that Jesus continually appeals to his title of "Son of Man" over and above the title of "Messiah." Bavinck also writes of this in his *Reformed Dogmatics*: "He did this in order to make clear both that he was the Messiah without whom the kingdom of God could not come and that he was the Messiah in a sense quite different from the way his contemporaries, in their earthbound expectations, pictured it. See *Reformed Dogmatics* III, 248–51; and Pass, *The Heart of Dogmatics*, 96n35.

5. See Bavinck, *Reformed Dogmatics* III, 323–417; and Bavinck, "De Persoon van Christus," *Handleiding bij het Onderwijs in den Christelijken Godsdienst*, 119–37.

6. It is worth noting that Bavinck should not be categorized as anti-Semitic. Van Klinken believes that Dutch Reformed theology was primarily interested in Judaism as it relates to eschatology and missions. See Gert van Klinken, "Herman Bavinck and Contemporary Judaism," lecture filmed at the Herman Bavinck Centennial Congress at Nieuwe Kerk, Kampen, November 12, 2021, https://www.youtube.com, 5:37–6:06. Bavinck's family was also involved in the anti-Nazi resistance movement; see Eglinton, *Bavinck: A Critical Biography* (Grand Rapids: Baker Academic, 2020), 297–98.

Chapter 3

1. Bavinck is referring to Gaius Plinius Secundus and Clement of Alexandria.

2. Bavinck's parenthetical depictions of both Ebionitism and Gnosticism obscure more than clarify his statement. The Dutch reads: "Ebionitisme (Judaïsme) en andererzijds die van het Gnosticisme (Ethnicisme)." Bracketed terms were added to clarify his meaning.

3. See Bavinck, *The Sacrifice of Praise*, trans. Cameron Clausing and Gregory Parker Jr. (Peabody, MA: Hendrickson, 2019), 30.

4. The categorizing of lower religions as polytheistic and the higher religions as monotheistic is appropriated from Schleiermacher. See Friedrich Schleiermacher, *The Christian Faith: A New Translation and Critical Edition*, trans. and ed. Catherine L. Kelsey, Terrence N. Tice, and Edwina Lawler (Louisville, KY: Westminster John Knox, 2016), §8; See Pass, "Introduction," 18–20.

5. See Bavinck, *Handleiding bij het Onderwijs in den Christelijken Godsdienst*, 121.

6. See Bavinck, *Christian Worldview*, trans. and ed. James Eglinton, Cory Brock, and Nathaniel Sutanto (Wheaton, IL: Crossway, 2019).

7. See Bavinck, *The Sacrifice of Praise*, 51–57.

8. It should be noted that Bavinck is *describing* the Russian church, not *prescribing* what he perceives to be a correct union of religion and life. To some degree, these words written in 1912 should startle the reader as they anticipate the atrocities carried out against the Jews in Soviet Russia (see also ch. 2, endnote 6 above), in addition to the pogroms already perpetrated by the Russian Empire (1881–1884 and 1903–1906).

9. This is the only known place where Bavinck utilizes the phrase "*mystieken cultus*" or "mystical cult." In *Reformed Dogmatics* I, 148, he provides a description of "mystical theology" that may shed some light: "The object of mystical theology, however, is the mystical communion with God granted by special grace to a small number of privileged persons. Mysticism describes how and by what way the soul could attain to such communion with God and what light could be shed on the truths of faith from that vantage point. In that sense mysticism has always had its representatives in the Christian church and occurs in greater or lesser measure in all the church fathers." In this context, Bavinck describes the Eastern Orthodox as mystical in their religious practices (particularly, their veneration of icons).

10. This section is a telling line for how Bavinck understands Catholic thought. He views Rome as making space for naturally good works to have natural rather than supernatural ends. He thought this often led to dualism in Catholic thought. See Gregory Parker Jr., "Reformation or Revolution? Herman Bavinck and Henri de Lubac on Nature and Grace," *Perichoresis* 15, no. 3 (2017): 81–95.

11. See Gregory the Great, *The Book of Pastoral Rule: St. Gregory the Great* (Yonkers, NY: St. Vladimirs Seminary Press, 2007).

Chapter 4

1. "For in it the righteousness of God is revealed from faith for faith, as it is written, 'The righteous shall live by faith'" (Rom. 1:17).

2. Bavinck seems to have in mind here Luther's more radical set of ninety-seven theses titled "Disputation against Scholastic Theology." Luther delivered this set of theses on September 4, 1517, at the University of Wittenberg. It is unclear if Bavinck simply meant to write "Ninety-Seven," or if he intended to provide the climatic date of October 31, 1517 (see also *Reformed Dogmatics* III, 517–19).

3. In April 1529, the Imperial Free Cities petitioned against the ban on Luther and called for the allowance of the Protestant faith (see *Reformed Dogmatics* IV, 368).

4. See Heinrich Denifle, *Luther and Lutherdom*, trans. Raymund Volz (Somerset: Torch Press, 1917).

5. In Abraham Kuyper's *Encyclopaedie*, he places several figures into the paradigm of "fathers" or "doctors" of the church. Kuyper likewise suggests Luther is a *pater ecclesia* of the Lutheran Church. See Kuyper, *Encyclopaedie der heilige Godgeleerdheid*, 3 vols. (Amsterdam: J. A. Worsmer, 1894), III, 389. See also James Eglinton, "The Reception of Aquinas in Kuyper's *Encyclopaedie der heilige Godgeleerdheid*," in *The Oxford Handbook of the Reception of Aquinas*, ed. Matthew Levering and Marcus Plested (Oxford: Oxford University Press, 2021), 452–66, 464.

6. See Bavinck, "The Influence of the Protestant Reformation on the Moral and Religious Condition of Communities and Nations" (1892), Box 346, Folder 345, Herman Bavinck Archive, Vrije Universiteit Amsterdam, Amsterdam, Netherlands, 1–19. In a speech delivered in 1892 to the General Council of Toronto, Bavinck talked about the relationship between Catholic, Lutheran, and Calvinist first principles in a similar fashion.

Chapter 6

1. Catholic scholar Louis Massignon (1883–1962) attributed the beginning of the "Three Imposter" legend to Abû Tâhir Sulaymân (907–944). See Louis Massignon, "La légende de tribus impostoribus et ses origines islamiques," in *Revue de l'Histoire des Religions*, deel 82, 1920, 74–78. The

tract was distributed in various forms in the Middle Ages attributing the "Three Imposters" to be the founders of the three monotheistic religions (Moses, Jesus, and Muhammad).

2. By 1912, when Bavinck published *Het Christendom*, he was simultaneously a lecturer at the *Vrije Universiteit* and a sitting member of the First Chamber of the Dutch Parliament. During this time, Bavinck delivered several speeches related to Dutch colonial expansion. These speeches offer some historical background to Bavinck's somewhat problematic and polemical statements above. In Bavinck's speech on December 29, 1911, he saw Western culture and Christianity as inseparable. In this speech, he attempted to distinguish Western culture and Christianity with the intention of bringing them back together again. He believed they could not simply export Western culture without in the end dehumanizing the people of the East. He repeated the claims of James Bryce that "if then they are offered nothing but culture, they will be deprived of more than they have possessed and their last will be worse than their first." In particular, he believed that if they exported Western culture without Christianity, it would ultimately lead former, now-secularized confessors of Islam and Buddhism to not only reject Western culture but also to despise its religion (see 29 December 1911, *Verslag der Handelingen van de Eerste Kamer*, 126–28). In a later speech on January 7, 1914, Bavinck—among other concerns relating to the exporting of religion and culture—articulated a similar view but reframed it as an international concern. In other words, it was an issue of maintaining the preservation of Western civilization vis-à-vis Eastern civilization. He called for a united Christian front to partake in this mission to, in some way, lift up these lower religions (see ch. 3, endnote 4 above). Two things are worth noting. First, was not religion per se that he emphasized but rather the superior ethical, intellectual, and social principles of Christianity. Within the walls of Christianity we do see a more ecumenical Bavinck. Second, he did suggest that if in the end the Dutch people had exported both their culture and Christianity, and the people of those colonies remained or became Islamic or Buddhists, the Dutch mission will not have been a failure. This interesting caveat seems to offer some room for negotiating Bavinck's exact understandings of stepping into pluralism. In the end, Bavinck viewed these other religions as troubling on account of the impact he anticipated that they might have on Western culture. (See 7 January 1914, *Verslag der Handelingen van de Eerste Kamer*, 119–22; and Eglinton, *Bavinck*, 265) Implicitly, then, he worried about the impact these other religions would have not only on Western culture but, in the end, on Christianity itself.

The Christian Faith

1. Later in his life, Bavinck wrote a book that directly introduces readers to the topic of confession. See *The Sacrifice of Praise*, trans. and ed. Cameron Clausing and Gregory Parker Jr. (Peabody, MA: Hendrickson, 2019)).

2. Here Bavinck is illustrating the idea that those unacquainted with Christ will allow for the existence of God, heaven, and hell, etc., as it suits them. God does not simply exist; they must vote him into existence. For example, the US Senate requires a majority (51 votes of 100) to pass a bill. Likewise, the Dutch Senate made decisions by majority (see *The Constitution of the Netherlands*, art. 67, 87).

SUBJECT INDEX